OUR
SPIRITUAL
ENEMIES

To Todd,

All of our earthly trials,
are only Spiritual Opportunities.

Paul Zybura

OUR SPIRITUAL ENEMIES

THE WORLD, THE FLESH, AND THE DEVIL

PAUL V. ZYLSTRA

Print ISBN: 978-0-9994887-2-0
E-Book ISBN: 978-0-9994887-3-7

Published and printed in the United States of America by the Write Place, Inc.
For more information, please contact:

the Write Place, Inc.
809 W. 8th Street, Suite 2
Pella, Iowa 50219
www.thewriteplace.biz

Cover and interior design by Michelle Stam, the Write Place, Inc.

Bible quotations in this book are from the King James Version of the Bible unless otherwise indicated.

Copies of this book may be ordered online at Amazon and BarnesandNoble.com.

View other Write Place titles at www.thewriteplace.biz.

DEDICATION

This book is dedicated to my good friend and first great Bible teacher, Warren Rushton. Most of this material is just a rearrangement of his teachings.

TABLE OF CONTENTS

PART 3 -VICTORY ABOVE THE BATTLE

PREFACE

AS HUMAN BEINGS, we look at everything around us in terms of our senses: what we see, what we touch, what we smell, what we hear, and what we taste. Our understanding depends upon our ability to experience life. The fewer senses we have available, the less ability we have to navigate through the physical obstacles of life. We are truly physical creatures with physical needs that relate to physical aspirations about life in general. When we experience life we seldom relate it to a spiritual realm that we cannot see.

As Christians, we must realize that what we sense is not all that there is. There are forces at work beyond our senses that we have trouble recognizing. These would include angels, demons, and even God Himself. These things still exist, but they are outside of our ability to sense them directly, unless they reveal themselves to us. Almighty God has done this in several ways. We have Jesus Christ, the "Immanuel" or "God with us" (Matthew 1:23, Isaiah 7:14). Jesus' own example of dealing with the realm that we do not see is very useful for us. He has given His written Word to anyone who will care to read it. For the Christian believer, Jesus has also sent us the Holy Spirit to guide and direct us. Even so, our ability to experience God and His loving kindness is limited by our physical, time-oriented, three-dimensional universe.

Not all the activities in the spiritual realm are actively promoting the goodness of God. A battleground exists at the point where the spirit world meets the physical world. The believer has Spiritual Enemies that the Bible declares, yet we cannot perceive them as spiritual through our physical senses. Because of this limitation, God must fight this battle for us. We are required to be sober minded concerning these battles (1 Peter 1:13), yet we are often like Job, who did not realize that the Devil was the real source of his earthly physical conflicts (Job Chapters 1 through 3). As a result, even when we recognize the spiritual battle, we often wrongfully approach it in physical terms believing that the spirit world has the same limitations and physical attributes that we have. What fools we are in our own human frailty to think that we can overcome a far superior force of Heaven by our own efforts or merits. The ultimate weapon for defeating ALL our Spiritual Enemies is the very physical and real Cross of Jesus Christ. The "once for all time sacrifice" of our Lord and Savior is the only means by which we may be spared the ravages of sin. For the Christian, the physical enemy is Sin in all its forms; but the Spiritual Enemies influencing the physical world hold great sway in their encouragement of our evil activity.

This book details the biblical study of our Spiritual Enemies: the World, the Flesh, and the Devil. Not only will these enemies be examined, but our defenses against them as well. Victory over sin is possible by the Blood of Jesus Christ, but it may help to understand the temptations that all of us face, why we face them, and what we can do to overcome them. It will soon be discovered that we have absolutely no ability in ourselves to overcome any of these enemies of our soul. God has already provided the solution, and all we can do is recognize His leading in our lives to overcome any and all spiritual obstacles.

Many may wonder at all of this, thinking that spiritual warfare is somehow pointless. Actually, God allows all of His children to be tested for their benefit.

*2 My brethren, count it all joy when ye fall into divers temptations;
3 Knowing this, that the trying of your faith worketh patience. 4 But
let patience have her perfect work, that ye may be perfect and entire,
wanting nothing. JAMES 1:2-4 (KJV)*

God even uses our enemies to our benefit. Our spiritual battles are what prepare us for eternity future. This is our boot camp for the eternal service of our Lord.

Paul V. Zylstra

November 2017

PART ONE

THE BATTLE

A Mighty Fortress Is Our God

Text: Martin Luther, trans. by Frederick H. Hedge
Music: Martin Luther Harmony
Tune: EIN' FESTE BURG

1. A mighty fortress is our God,
   a bulwark never failing;
   our helper he amid the flood
   of mortal ills prevailing.
   For still our ancient foe
   doth seek to work us woe;
   his craft and power are great,
   and armed with cruel hate,
   on earth is not his equal.

2. Did we in our own strength confide,
   our striving would be losing,
   were not the right man on our side,
   the man of God's own choosing.
   Dost ask who that may be?
   Christ Jesus, it is he;
   Lord Sabaoth, his name,
   from age to age the same,
   and he must win the battle.

3. And though this world, with devils filled,
   should threaten to undo us,
   we will not fear, for God hath willed
   His truth to triumph through us.
   The Prince of Darkness grim,
   we tremble not for him;
   his rage we can endure,
   for lo, his doom is sure;
   one little word shall fell him.

4. That word above all earthly powers,
   no thanks to them, abideth;
   the Spirit and the gifts are ours,
   thru him who with us sideth.
   Let goods and kindred go,
   this mortal life also;
   the body they may kill;
   God's truth abideth still;
   His kingdom is forever.

CHAPTER ONE

WHAT IS SPIRITUAL WARFARE?

"A MIGHTY FORTRESS IS OUR GOD" was written by Martin Luther sometime prior to his excommunication from the Roman Catholic Church. It was written around Psalm 47. The song is known as the "Battle Hymn of the Reformation." It has been translated into almost every language. Luther was hunted as a heretic, hated by the powerful of the Roman Catholic Church, and condemned for his faithfulness to God and His Word. Even so, Luther did not consider humanity to be his enemy. As the song relates, the enemy of Luther and the Reformation was and is the Devil. In the first verse, Luther wrote about our refuge in God from our mighty oppressor the Devil. In the second verse, Luther recognizes that we are no match for this enemy of our souls, but God has supplied for us a champion that the Devil cannot defeat, Christ Jesus. In the third verse, Luther addresses our warfare with the entire Satanic World System and declares our inevitable victory. In the last verse, Luther describes the power that is available to the believer and the steadfastness of God regardless of circumstance, even death. The entirety of the Reformation was built around the unchanging nature of God and His personal care for the believer. Martin Luther understood the real battle and the real enemy. Luther was influenced to write his hymns by those who fell as martyrs for the cause of Christ, but Luther considered that their memory would be best served by considering the cause that gave strength to the fallen.[1] The true nature of the Gospel has always been in God's faithfulness to deliver the believer from sin, but the enemy is always putting traps, distractions, and temptations in our way in an effort to ruin Christian testimony and bring discredit to the Cross of Jesus Christ. That battle rages around us, but we seldom consider the source of the strength for the opposition as Luther did.

SPIRITUAL WARFARE

As with all wars, there are certain things that are common to the battle. You must have opposing elements. You must have a reason for opposition. You must have a location for battle ,or a battleground. You must have a means of defense, or one side would easily overwhelm the other. Generally, we think of opposing elements as either meeting face to face or at least along defined battle lines, but what if these battle lines are invisible? What is more, what if the enemy is invisible? Even worse, what if the enemy is not perceived as an enemy at all, or may not even exist? In fact, what if our warfare starts with all of us in league with the enemy and on the wrong side of the battle, and the only means of being spared is to defect to the other side? What if that defection defies logic because it requires us to recognize that we have no means of defense in the battle on our own? And what if such a defection alienates us from our friends, our environment, and our future prospects for perceived acceptance and advancement? What if that defection consigns us to a life of testing, turmoil, and tribulation because we are outside the realm of what is acceptable and desire to live outside of the enemy camp? What if we proceed into that battle without any hope in ourselves, and yet believing that an invisible enemy will be defeated for us by a superior invisible battle force whose plans we are not entirely privy to, but whose commander and commands we accept without the benefit of even knowing anything other than that He will do whatever it takes to deliver us in the battle if we will only trust Him to do so? What if defeat for us can only come if we fail to trust the commander and His leading, or if we listen to and accept the lying propaganda of the enemy, or if we are enticed by others who have not defected, or if we love the enemy more than we love the commander?

This pretty much describes our situation in spiritual warfare. The battle is fought over sin. The sinner is in the midst of the battle and we perceive temptation to sin as coming from our physical surroundings, but it actually originates from the Devil, or his world system, as a test of our faith. The battle ground is at the point where the spiritual realm and the physical realm meet; in the heart of the individual. The foes are not those who openly oppose the good news of Jesus Christ. The foe is the enemy of our souls, the Devil. We are all sinners who start out on the wrong side of the battle until we are saved by God's grace. We come into this world serving a master that we cannot see and may not even believe to exist. His name is Satan and the Devil. This battle is summed up for us in the book of Ephesians:

> 10 Finally, my brethren, be strong in the Lord, and in the power of his might. 11 Put on the whole armour of God, that ye may be able to stand against the wiles of the devil. 12 For we wrestle not against flesh and blood, but against principalities, against powers, against the rulers of the darkness of this world, against spiritual wickedness in high places. EPHESIANS 6:10-12 (KJV)

As Christians, we look at our problems as earthly, three dimensional, and highly influenced by the actions of others. For sure other people play a major role in actions and decision making. Some may tempt us through flattery and great success, while others tempt us through persecution, lies, and treachery. The real source of the temptation does not rest with humanity. The source is spiritual in nature.

KNOW THE ENEMY

There are three enemies that the believer must deal with daily. One is within the individual and the others are outside of, or without, the individual.

THE FLESH

The first spiritual enemy is self, or more specifically the sin nature that dwells within us all. In Chapter 2, we will deal with our own sin nature and find that it can only be controlled by the Spirit of God. Not even an external restraint of law is a substitute for the controlling power of the Holy Spirit.

THE DEVIL

The second spiritual enemy is Satan, or the Devil. In Chapter 3, we look at the history of Satan, the sphere of Satan's influence, the power of Satan, the temptations of Satan, and God's purpose for these temptations. It will be evident that we are no match for this ancient foe, but God provides supernatural remedies for our support.

THE WORLD

The third spiritual enemy is the Satanic World System. In Chapter 4, we look at the relationship between the World and the Devil and discover that the World receives its power and influence primarily by means of Satan. We look at the World as a spiritual enemy from without and at what God has provided as a defense against the World.

These enemies of our souls encompass that battle and it rages all around us. At stake is our fellowship with God. As we try to achieve victory over sin by natural means (that is LAW), we alienate ourselves from the Grace of God. Soon we find ourselves without strength to overcome sin and thus lose fellowship with God because of that sin. The more we yield to and trust God by faith, the closer our fellowship with Him and the better our protection from our spiritual enemy, both within and without.

SPIRITUALITY AND SPIRITUAL MATURITY

The degree of individual spirituality is at issue, but not in the sense of length of time saved. If the individual is saved, all the benefits of salvation are available regardless of how long or how short the time that the individual has been saved. Nor is it a question of knowledge. Though knowledge helps, God does not withhold His assistance because of our ignorance. He is still gracious towards the believer, but God still abhors our sin. In contrast to spirituality, no believer is instantaneously mature as a Christian; it is obviously a lifetime pursuit. The more the individual yields to God's leading, the closer the fellowship with God. It is faith and not knowledge that determines both spirituality and maturity. A Christian with a minimal IQ can be every bit as spiritual as a Christian genius. Faith does have content, but maturity is more a matter of faith and dependence on God than it is on academic excellence, quickness of wit, or length of service. Maturity does depend, to an extent, upon an understanding of God as revealed in the Bible, but knowledge never outweighs faith. For maturity, God provides believers with the assistance of others whom He has specially equipped for that purpose.

11 And he gave some, apostles; and some, prophets; and some, evangelists; and some, pastors and teachers; 12 For the perfecting of the saints, for the work of the ministry, for the edifying of the body of Christ: 13 Till we all come in the unity of the faith, and of the knowledge of the Son of God, unto a perfect man, unto the measure of the stature of the fulness of Christ: 14 That we henceforth be no more children, tossed to and fro, and carried about with every wind of doctrine, by the sleight of men, and cunning craftiness, whereby they lie in wait to deceive; 15 But speaking the truth in love, may grow up into him in all things, which is the head, even Christ: EPHESIANS 4:11-15 (KJV)

The word for "perfect" in verse 13 is **teleios,** and it means "mature" or all "grown up."[2] The idea of maturing gradually in our Christian walk is known theologically as "progressive sanctification." For this, God supplies the help of others in the way of pastors, teachers, and evangelists. The goal is to become more like Christ. This implies much more than just knowledge. More than anything spirituality and maturity imply a developing relationship and a gaining of trust with God. Unfortunately, there are those Christians who never seem to grow in their faith and the Bible specifically addresses them.

12 Now we have received, not the spirit of the world, but the spirit which is of God; that we might know the things that are freely given to us of God. 13 Which things also we speak, not in the words which man's wisdom teacheth, but which the Holy Ghost teacheth; comparing spiritual things with spiritual. 14 But the natural man receiveth not the things of the Spirit of God: for they are foolishness unto him: neither can he know them, because they are spiritually discerned. 15 But he that is spiritual judgeth all things, yet he himself is judged of no man. 16 For who hath known the mind of the Lord, that he may instruct him? But we have the mind of Christ. 3 And I, brethren, could not speak unto you as unto spiritual, but as unto carnal, even as unto babes in Christ. 2 I have fed you with milk, and not with meat: for hitherto ye were not able to bear it, neither yet now are ye able. 3 For ye are yet carnal: for whereas there is among you envying, and strife, and divisions, are ye not carnal, and walk as men? 1 CORINTHIANS 2:12-3:3 (KJV)

This passage recognizes three different types of individuals: the unsaved natural man, the saved spiritual man, and the saved carnal (as opposed to spiritual) man. The unsaved man can know nothing of God because he does not have the Holy Spirit that is received at salvation. The spiritual man not only is assisted by the Holy Spirit, but he also has the mind of Christ to know the deep things of God. This apparently developed as his relationship to the Lord developed. The carnal Christian may be saved, but he remains a babe in Christ who has little desire to develop a relationship to the Lord. Note that the Spiritual man need not be brilliant on his own because God provides him with the mind of Christ to know the deep things of God. The fact that the babe in Christ is described as "carnal," or fleshly, indicates that this Christian is caught up in some kind of sin. As will be seen, carnality is synonymous with an active sin nature. This sin prevents the Christian from being sanctified to the Lord. He is stumbled in his relationship to the Lord and cannot grow in his faith. Everything is still available to him to get out of that condition, but he is languishing in his sin. The latter part of the passage would suggest that his attitude was a primary reason for carnality. The carnal Christian very much needs to develop his relationship with the Lord in order to enjoy a victorious Christian life. This group would concede the battle were it not for the Spirit of God ministering grace to them.

THE TRAP OF LEGALISM

There are other hindrances to spirituality and maturity, such as a reliance on legalistic principles, rather than a direct reliance on God and His grace. Many Churches preach salvation by grace, only to have people live by law instead of the same grace wherein they were saved. It is amazing how many pastors are ignorant of God's present work of salvation in the believer's life, yet a life of grace is the goal.

> 11 For the grace of God that bringeth salvation hath appeared to all
> men, 12 Teaching us that, denying ungodliness and worldly lusts, we
> should live soberly, righteously, and godly, in this present world; 13
> Looking for that blessed hope, and the glorious appearing of the great

God and our Saviour Jesus Christ; 14 Who gave himself for us, that he
might redeem us from all iniquity, and purify unto himself a peculiar
people, zealous of good works. TITUS 2:11-14 (KJV)

If the passage above teaches anything it is that the saving grace of
God teaches us how to live until the future appearance of the Lord. The
last verse explicitly states that our ability to live and serve is a result of
the redeeming work of Jesus Christ on the cross. This is the opposite
of legalism, which seeks to earn the favor of God by obeying certain
Biblical principles in one's own strength instead of by the power of God.
The legalist substitutes self-effort and self-will for the continuous and
supernatural salvation of God by grace through faith. As a result, this
group of Christians is like Don Quixote, attacking windmills thinking
they are giants to be slain. They mistakenly think that the battle is Earthly
instead of Spiritual. The result is a defeated and exhausted believer who
is thoroughly confused. He tries to do all the right things in his own
strength rather than relying on the leading of the Lord. These believers
want to redefine the battle in earthly terms with very little understanding
of the actual enemy. This group often insists that they are never tempted
by the Devil as a spiritual enemy.

A WORD ABOUT PSYCHOLOGY

If the term "psychology" is broken down to its component parts we see
that **psychos** is the Greek word for "soul," and **ology** means "the study of."
Psychology is therefore "the Study of the Soul" or a "study of the soulish
man." From the three types of individuals declared in 1 Corinthians,
this would be the study of the "natural man." A study of the "Spiritual
Life" and a study of "Psychology" both address the immaterial parts of
man. Some of the component parts are common to both areas of study
such as the "Will" and the "Conscience." Psychology is limited in its

approach in that it relates everything to the physical world and avoids any connection to either a creator God or the enemy of our souls, the Devil. Psychology looks at cause-and-effect relationships for behavior, but does not recognize the fallen, sin nature of man as an underlying cause. We know that we all have this indwelling sin nature:

12 *Wherefore, as by one man sin entered into the world, and death by sin; and so death passed upon all men, for that all have sinned:*
ROMANS 5:12 (KJV)

This is a universal problem for man:

23 *For all have sinned, and come short of the glory of God;*
ROMANS 3:23 (KJV)

Psychology only looks at external influences for behavior; therefore, man is never a stand-alone sinner. Man is always in a state of becoming something or evolving. External influences may or may not be viewed as temptations, but these influences are never credited to an unseen being like the Devil. Nor is the influencing world considered to be controlled or even influenced by the Devil.

Psychology also tries to normalize as much human behavior as is possible, including divorce, remarriage, homosexuality, and other behaviors that God has declared in the Bible to be sin. Other more abhorrent behaviors are declared to be illnesses or addictions, such as gambling, pedophilia, theft (kleptomania), drunkenness (alcoholism), or drug use.

Psychology cannot accept the absolute nature of anything, nor can it accept the existence and control of an absolute God. As such psychology has an incomplete model of man and his behavior. This book presents the Spiritual Life as a battle between "good" and "evil," with the battle taking place in the battleground of the mind. This book is for the select audience of the believing. Only the Spiritual, or Saved, individual can understand it because all of it depends upon the supernatural intervention of an all-powerful, all-knowing, everywhere-present and loving Creator God.

THIS IS THE BATTLE!

CHAPTER TWO

OUR SPIRITUAL ENEMY–THE FLESH

THIS CHAPTER WILL DEFINE THE FLESH as a Spiritual Enemy and point to what the Bible declares to be the remedy for overcoming this enemy. There is also interdependence between the enemies of God, and they are not independent from one another. Nowhere is this better seen than in the origins of sin.

THE FALL OF MAN

Man was created in the image of God. This fact makes man not only unique among all the creatures on Earth, but in Heaven as well. Not even the angels are said to be created in the image of God.

26 And God said, Let us make man in our image, after our likeness: and let them have dominion over the fish of the sea, and over the fowl of the air, and over the cattle, and over all the earth, and over every creeping thing that creepeth upon the earth. 27 So God created man in his own image, in the image of God created he him; male and female created he them. 28 And God blessed them, and God said unto them, Be fruitful, and multiply, and replenish the earth, and subdue it: and have dominion over the fish of the sea, and over the fowl of the air, and over every living thing that moveth upon the earth. GENESIS 1:26-28 (KJV)

Man was also created innocent and without sin. Even though God knew that the free moral agent that he created would eventually fall into rebellion against Him, God gave man every opportunity to succeed on his own. God had only one requirement for his newly created creature man:

16 And the Lord God commanded the man, saying, Of every tree of the garden thou mayest freely eat: 17 But of the tree of the knowledge of good and evil, thou shalt not eat of it: for in the day that thou eatest thereof thou shalt surely die. GENESIS 2:16-17 (KJV)

Man may have been content in his innocence had God not allowed the Devil in the form of a serpent to tempt Eve, the first woman. This was mankind's first temptation by the enemy without called the Devil. The temptation is recounted as follows:

1 Now the serpent was more subtil than any beast of the field which the Lord God had made. And he said unto the woman, Yea, hath God said, Ye shall not eat of every tree of the garden? 2 And the woman said unto the serpent, We may eat of the fruit of the trees of the garden: 3 But of the fruit of the tree which is in the midst of the garden, God hath said, Ye shall not eat of it, neither shall ye touch it, lest ye die. 4 And the serpent said unto the woman, Ye shall not surely die: 5 For God doth know that in the day ye eat thereof, then your eyes shall be opened, and ye shall be as gods, knowing good and evil. 6 And when the woman saw that the tree was good for food, and that it was pleasant to the eyes, and a tree to be desired to make one wise, she took of the fruit thereof, and did eat, and gave also unto her husband with her; and he did eat. 7 And the eyes of them both were opened, and they knew that they were naked; and they sewed fig leaves together, and made themselves aprons. GENESIS 3:1-7 (KJV)

The appeal of that fruit must have been very strong. The fact that it was good for food had a practical appeal, but the fact that it was pleasant to the eye made the fruit something that we today would have singled out to put in our shopping cart. It was easy for the Devil to sell the idea of eating the fruit because it had what would be referred to today as "market appeal." This is true of most sensual sin. The thing that really attracted man to sin was that he could become as smart as God, knowing good and evil. There is no indication that man understood good and evil before the fall and every indication that man had no idea what it was. It was the sales pitch (or lie) of the Devil that made the idea so attractive. Several things happened when man decided to ignore the commandment of God:

1. The Man and the Woman lost innocence as evidenced by the fact that they knew they were naked.

2. The Man and the Woman obtained a conscience; that is, an understanding of good and evil.

3. The Man and the Woman also obtained a sin nature that eventually distorted their view of right and wrong.

4. Man could no longer abide the presence of a Holy God as is evidenced by the verses that followed.

8 And they heard the voice of the Lord God walking in the garden in the cool of the day: and Adam and his wife hid themselves from the presence of the Lord God amongst the trees of the garden. 9 And the Lord God called unto Adam, and said unto him, Where art thou? 10 And he said, I heard thy voice in the garden, and I was afraid, because I was naked; and I hid myself. GENESIS 3:8-11 (KJV)

As God had promised the punishment was quite severe.

11 And he said, Who told thee that thou wast naked? Hast thou eaten of the tree, whereof I commanded thee that thou shouldest not eat? 12 And the man said, The woman whom thou gavest to be with me, she gave me of the tree, and I did eat. 13 And the Lord God said unto the woman, What is this that thou hast done? And the woman said, The serpent beguiled me, and I did eat. 14 And the Lord God said unto the serpent, Because thou hast done this, thou art cursed above all cattle, and above every beast of the field; upon thy belly shalt thou go, and dust shalt thou eat all the days of thy life: 15 And I will put enmity between thee and the woman, and between thy seed and her seed; it shall bruise thy head, and thou shalt bruise his heel. 16 Unto the woman he said, I will greatly multiply thy sorrow and thy conception; in sorrow thou shalt bring forth children; and thy desire shall be to thy husband, and he shall rule over thee. 17 And unto Adam he said, Because thou hast hearkened unto the voice of thy wife, and hast eaten of the tree, of which I commanded thee, saying, Thou shalt not eat of it: cursed is the ground for thy sake; in sorrow shalt thou eat of it all the days of thy life; 18 Thorns also and thistles shall it bring forth to thee; and thou shalt eat the herb of the field; 19 In the sweat of thy face shalt thou eat bread, till thou return unto the ground; for out of it wast thou taken: for dust thou art, and unto dust shalt thou return. GENESIS 3:11-19 (KJV)

Built into the curse placed upon man was a promise of deliverance through the seed of the woman to defeat the Devil in verse 15. As will be seen, sin was overcome at the Cross of Jesus Christ many thousands of years later.

THE FLESH - THE ENEMY WITHIN

The Flesh is another term for the "sin nature" that we all inherited from our parents, going all the way back to our father Adam at the fall of man in the Garden of Eden.

> *12 Wherefore, as by one man sin entered into the world, and death by sin; and so death passed upon all men, for that all have sinned: ROMANS 5:12 (KJV)*

The Flesh is an enemy within every man and it is an enemy of God:

> *17 For the flesh lusteth against the Spirit, and the Spirit against the flesh: and these are contrary the one to the other: so that ye cannot do the things that ye would. GALATIANS 5:17 (KJV)*

Those who do not know the saving grace of God through the finished work of Jesus Christ on Calvary's Cross are doomed to live and dwell in their sinful desires. The results of fleshly desire are known in the Bible as the "Works of the Flesh."

> *19 Now the works of the flesh are manifest, which are these; Adultery, fornication, uncleanness, lasciviousness, 20 Idolatry, witchcraft, hatred, variance, emulations, wrath, strife, seditions, heresies, 21 Envyings, murders, drunkenness, revellings, and such like: of the which I tell you before, as I have also told you in time past, that they which do such things shall not inherit the kingdom of God. GALATIANS 5:19-21 (KJV)*

Each of these evil things could be a study on its own, and unfortunately it is not exhaustive as the phrase "and such like" would indicate.

Individual "Works of the Flesh" will be addressed in a later chapter. The ability for man to sin is only limited by his imagination to conceive of sin. Every one of us is powerless to overcome our own internal desire to sin, but the Lord has provided a means for us to overcome the Flesh with its sinful desires and evil works.

6 Knowing this, that our old man is crucified with him, that the body of sin might be destroyed, that henceforth we should not serve sin. 7 For he that is dead is freed from sin. 8 Now if we be dead with Christ, we believe that we shall also live with him: 9 Knowing that Christ being raised from the dead dieth no more; death hath no more dominion over him. 10 For in that he died, he died unto sin once: but in that he liveth, he liveth unto God. 11 Likewise reckon ye also yourselves to be dead indeed unto sin, but alive unto God through Jesus Christ our Lord. ROMANS 6:6-11 (KJV)

THE INTERNAL RESTRAINT OF THE SPIRIT

Jesus paid our debt of sin: past, present, and future.

4 Surely he hath borne our griefs, and carried our sorrows: yet we did esteem him stricken, smitten of God, and afflicted. 5 But he was wounded for our transgressions, he was bruised for our iniquities: the chastisement of our peace was upon him; and with his stripes we are healed. 6 All we like sheep have gone astray; we have turned every one to his own way; and the Lord hath laid on him the iniquity of us all. ISAIAH 53:4-6 (KJV)

Not only did He pay the price for the sins that we commit, but he also has made it possible for each of us to escape the power of sin in our own lives. The sin nature (or Flesh) that dwells within each of us is nailed to the cross with our Savior. Because of the complete and finished work of

Jesus on the cross we can be free from our sinful desires. The one who superintends this freedom is the Holy Spirit.

> 16 This I say then, Walk in the Spirit, and ye shall not fulfil the lust of the flesh. GALATIANS 5:16 (KJV)

Notice that the impetus to overcome the Flesh is not on man. The authority to overcome sin belongs to God alone. The way that the sentence is constructed in the original language, the "shall not" comes from a double negative in the Greek combination **ou me,** with the negatives reinforcing one another.[1] It should be translated "absolutely cannot." It is obvious that the Holy Spirit is the only absolute means of overcoming sin. The means that the Holy Spirit uses to overcome the Flesh is not to change circumstances. Instead, the Spirit of God provides us with a whole new set of God-given attitudes.

> 22 But the fruit of the Spirit is love, joy, peace, longsuffering, gentleness, goodness, faith, 23 Meekness, temperance: against such there is no law. GALATIANS 5:22-23 (KJV)

Thus, as we yield to the control of the Holy Spirit we may live in fellowship with God regardless of the circumstances because the Spirit of God is in control. The attitudes listed as "Fruit of the Spirit" are given by God to the believer. They are not attitudes that we manufacture on our own. They are of the Spirit for man and not attitudes that we produce on our own to please God. This too is a result of the Cross of Jesus Christ.

> 24 And they that are Christ's have crucified the flesh with the affections and lusts. 25 If we live in the Spirit, let us also walk in the Spirit. GALATIANS 5:24-25 (KJV)

The attitudes listed as the "Fruit of the Spirit" will be described in more detail in Chapter 8.

THE EXTERNAL RESTRAINT OF THE LAW

The Holy Spirit acts as an internal restraint concerning sin. The Law of Moses was given as an external restraint to deter man from sinning. The Mosaic Law never saved anyone, nor can we be perfected through the law. The law requires the submission of our flesh to the righteousness of God. It does not come about without some kind of human rebellion. But the law as a deterrent to sin is much different than the law as a means of salvation from sin. Even the unsaved can appear to be good but that does not make them saved. Therefore, the unsaved can exhibit the goodness of the law as an external restraint even though they are ignorant of God.

> *8 But we know that the law is good, if a man use it lawfully; 9 Knowing this, that the law is not made for a righteous man, but for the lawless and disobedient, for the ungodly and for sinners, for unholy and profane, for murderers of fathers and murderers of mothers, for manslayers, 10 For whoremongers, for them that defile themselves with mankind, for menstealers, for liars, for perjured persons, and if there be any other thing that is contrary to sound doctrine; 11 According to the glorious gospel of the blessed God, which was committed to my trust. 1 TIMOTHY 1:8-11 (KJV)*

Even though the Apostle Paul started out talking about the Mosaic Law in the passage above, verse 8 is broader than the Mosaic Law and applies to the qualifications for any law principle. Even where God's moral law is not recognized, man places upon himself some law principle to act as an external restraint to protect society.

13 (For not the hearers of the law are just before God, but the doers of the law shall be justified. 14 For when the Gentiles, which have not the law, do by nature the things contained in the law, these, having not the law, are a law unto themselves: 15 Which shew the work of the law written in their hearts, their conscience also bearing witness, and their thoughts the mean while accusing or else excusing one another;) ROMANS 2:13-15 (KJV)

Those who have not placed their faith in Jesus and His finished work on the Cross do not have the internal restraint of the Spirit to overcome their sins. Those who do not believe are only restrained by the external restraint of law. This is why the Apostle Paul speaks of the law as being a schoolmaster to bring us up to the point of Christ.

23 But before faith came, we were kept under the law, shut up unto the faith which should afterwards be revealed. 24 Wherefore the law was our schoolmaster to bring us unto Christ, that we might be justified by faith. GALATIANS 3:23-24 (KJV)

The law is a trainer of the conscience, even the conscience of the unsaved, to establish order. But it is an inferior means of control.

3:29 And if ye be Christ's, then are ye Abraham's seed, and heirs according to the promise. 4:1 Now I say, That the heir, as long as he is a child, differeth nothing from a servant, though he be lord of all; 2 But is under tutors and governors until the time appointed of the father. 3 Even so we, when we were children, were in bondage under the elements of the world: 4 But when the fulness of the time was come, God sent forth his Son, made of a woman, made under the law, 5 To redeem them that were under the law, that we might receive the adoption of sons. GALATIANS 3:29-4:5 (KJV)

The very next verse establishes the superior means of internal control by the Holy Spirit.

> *6 And because ye are sons, God hath sent forth the Spirit of his Son into your hearts, crying, Abba, Father. GALATIANS 4:6 (KJV)*

It is unfortunate that most believers do not realize that they need not bear the responsibility for overcoming personal sin on their own. Those who try to overcome sin on their own place themselves under the same external restraint of the law that applies to those outside the faith. When even the restraint of law is thrown off the result is sin.

> *4 Whosoever committeth sin transgresseth also the law: for sin is the transgression of the law. 1 JOHN 3:4 (KJV)*

Sin is acting without either internal or external restraint, and this lack of restraint is rebellion against God. We should be thankful that God has made provision through Jesus to allow us to escape sin in the flesh.

> *5 And ye know that he was manifested to take away our sins; and in him is no sin. 1 JOHN 3:5 (KJV)*

Even believers can throw off both the internal restrain of the Spirit and the external restraint of the law, but the real sin for the believer is throwing off the restraint of the Spirit and leaving fellowship with God. At that point, not even man's will can keep him from sinning, even as a believer.

WILLPOWER IS FUTILE

Even though believers have the advantage of having the ability to walk by the Holy Spirit, if they do not the results are not very good.

In his book *He That Is Spiritual*, Dr. Lewis Sperry Chafer puts some extra emphasis into Romans 7 to help the reader to understand the strength of the Flesh.

> 14 For we know that the law is spiritual: but I *(the old man)* am carnal, sold under sin. 15 For that which I *(the old)* do I *(the new)* allow not: for what I *(the new)* would, that do I *(the old)* not; but what I *(the new)* hate, that do I *(the old)*. 16 If then I *(the old)* do that which I *(the new)* would not, I consent unto the law *(or will of God for me)* that it is good. 17 Now then it is no more I *(the new)* that do it, but sin *(the old)* that dwelleth in me. 18 For I know that in me *(the old)* (that is, in my flesh,) dwelleth no good thing: for to will is present with me; but how to perform that which is good I find not. 19 For the good that I *(the new)* would I *(the old)* do not: but the evil which I *(the new)* would not, that I *(the old)* do. 20 Now if I *(the old)* do that I *(the new)* would not, it is no more I *(the new)* that do it, but sin *(the old)* that dwelleth in me. 21 I find then a law *(not the law of Moses)*, that, when I *(the new)* would do good, evil *(the old)* is present with me. 22 For I delight in the law of God after the inward man: 23 But I see another law in my members *(the old)*, warring against the law of my mind *(the new that delights in the law of God)*, and bringing me into captivity to the law of sin *(the old)* which is in my members. 24 O wretched *(Christian)* man that I am! who shall deliver me from the body of this death? ROMANS 7:14-24 (KJV WITH MODIFICATIONS BY CHAFER)[2]

So, if the Flesh is so strong and the Holy Spirit is the only one who can control the Flesh by means of giving us new attitudes, what is there to take us out of fellowship with God? The answer to this is that we have two more enemies without called the World and the Devil. These Spiritual Enemies will be addressed in subsequent chapters.

HOW TO WALK BY THE SPIRIT

It is obvious that the key to overcoming sin in the life of the believer is to allow the Holy Spirit to control his life. There are several things to keep in mind when contemplating this relationship:

1. The nature of God the Holy Spirit

2. Forgiveness and maintaining fellowship with God

3. How we live after we are saved

All of these things are critical to the believer in his Christian walk by the Spirit of God.

THE NATURE OF GOD THE HOLY SPIRIT

It is amazing to observe the misconceptions that people have about the Holy Spirit. The view of the Church concerning the Holy Spirit has become so distorted that many Baptists, Presbyterians, and other non-Pentecostal groups are afraid to even mention anything about the third member of the Godhead. Obviously, this has guaranteed the personal lack of victory over sin that most believers experience. The general view of the Holy Spirit (both Pentecostal and non-Pentecostal) is that He resembles something similar to either molasses that sticks all over you, or thick air that can presumably be cut with a knife, or gasohol that we get our tanks topped off with, or something else that the Bible has never related. The Holy Spirit is none of these things. The Holy Spirit is the person promised by Jesus to aid and comfort the believer after the Lord's departure.

16 And I will pray the Father, and he shall give you another Comforter,
that he may abide with you for ever; 17 Even the Spirit of truth; whom

the world cannot receive, because it seeth him not, neither knoweth
him: but ye know him; for he dwelleth with you, and shall be in you. 18
I will not leave you comfortless: I will come to you. JOHN 14:16-18 (KJV)

The Holy Spirit is our professor to teach us about Christ and His
teachings:

26 But the Comforter, which is the Holy Ghost, whom the Father will
send in my name, he shall teach you all things, and bring all things to
your remembrance, whatsoever I have said unto you. JOHN 14:26 (KJV)

Along with a teaching ministry the Holy Spirit also has a convicting
ministry:

7 Nevertheless I tell you the truth; It is expedient for you that I go away:
for if I go not away, the Comforter will not come unto you; but if I depart, I
will send him unto you. 8 And when he is come, he will reprove the world
of sin, and of righteousness, and of judgment: 9 Of sin, because they believe
not on me; 10 Of righteousness, because I go to my Father, and ye see me no
more; 11 Of judgment, because the prince of this world is judged. 12 I have
yet many things to say unto you, but ye cannot bear them now. 13 Howbeit
when he, the Spirit of truth, is come, he will guide you into all truth: for
he shall not speak of himself; but whatsoever he shall hear, that shall he
speak: and he will shew you things to come. 14 He shall glorify me: for
he shall receive of mine, and shall shew it unto you. JOHN 16:7-14 (KJV)

The Holy Spirit operates on the conscience of the believer to show
and verify the truth as received from Christ. The Holy Spirit is not some
impersonal force. He has a personality that can be grieved and he secures
us in the Lord until we are redeemed.

30 And grieve not the holy Spirit of God, whereby ye are sealed unto the day of redemption. EPHESIANS 4:30 (KJV)

Not only are we sealed, but the Holy Spirit is given as a down payment for our salvation:

13 In whom ye also trusted, after that ye heard the word of truth, the gospel of your salvation: in whom also after that ye believed, ye were sealed with that holy Spirit of promise, 14 Which is the earnest of our inheritance until the redemption of the purchased possession, unto the praise of his glory. EPHESIANS 1:13-14 (KJV)

The Holy Spirit is a being who makes our personal God a personal being who loves us and cares for us. When we are saved, we receive the person of the Holy Spirit. It is an all-or-none action, like turning on a light switch. You either have Him or you do not. We cannot receive more of Him or lose part of Him to have less of Him. The Holy Spirit is a gift that does not vary in any way (James 1:17). When Christians throw off the restraint of the Holy Spirit, His ministry is no longer through the believer to others. The ministry of the Holy Spirit is to the believer to get them back into fellowship with God.

FORGIVENESS AND MAINTAINING FELLOWSHIP WITH GOD

When we sin as Christians, we lose fellowship with God. Fellowship is regained the same way that we were saved in the first place. We must recognize our sin before God.

9 If we confess our sins, he is faithful and just to forgive us our sins, and to cleanse us from all unrighteousness. 1 JOHN 1:9 (KJV)

The term "confess" means to "say the same thing about."[3] Identifying and telling the truth about our sin is a condition for forgiveness, thus God's forgiveness is not unconditional. The purpose of forgiveness is also not one sided. The purpose is to restore our fellowship with God. It is unfortunate that forgiveness has been so modernized and distorted to imply that it is unilateral and unconditional. If this were the case, then Hell would be empty and everyone would be going to Heaven. Forgiveness is for reconciliation and restoration, and it is always conditioned on recognition of the truth about our sin. That is true repentance, not that we do something in the way of restitution to God. Jesus has already paid the price for our sin at the Cross. We must humbly cast ourselves at His feet, recognizing that we are sinners, and that we can do nothing to pay Him back for our sins. Because of the finished work of the Cross, Jesus pleads our case.

> *My little children, these things write I unto you, that ye sin not. And if any man sin, we have an advocate with the Father, Jesus Christ the righteous: 2 And he is the propitiation for our sins: and not for ours only, but also for the sins of the whole world. 1 JOHN 2:1-2 (KJV)*

Jesus has already paid the price for our sins completely at the Cross and need not do it again. Because of that, Jesus is our advocate if we trust and lean on him. The result is a restored fellowship with God that was not possible before the Cross.

HOW WE LIVE AFTER WE ARE SAVED

Our confession is a good thing and it will restore our fellowship with God, but if everything that follows was up to us we would get nothing done but our continual confession. Our ability to actually live apart from sin is a result of the Cross.

27

11 Likewise reckon ye also yourselves to be dead indeed unto sin, but alive unto God through Jesus Christ our Lord. 12 Let not sin therefore reign in your mortal body, that ye should obey it in the lusts thereof. 13 Neither yield ye your members as instruments of unrighteousness unto sin: but yield yourselves unto God, as those that are alive from the dead, and your members as instruments of righteousness unto God. 14 For sin shall not have dominion over you: for ye are not under the law, but under grace. ROMANS 6:11-14 (KJV)

Our sin nature (i.e. Flesh) was nailed to the Cross with Jesus. Because of this, we can consider ourselves dead to sin and alive to Christ. Thus, by the grace of God we are freed from sin. There is a passage of Scripture that is generally used as an initial salvation passage, but it has little if anything to do with initial salvation.

8 For by grace are ye saved through faith; and that not of yourselves: it is the gift of God: 9 Not of works, lest any man should boast. 10 For we are his workmanship, created in Christ Jesus unto good works, which God hath before ordained that we should walk in them. EPHESIANS 2:8-10 (KJV)

The "are" in verse 8 is a state of being verb in the present indicative tense.[4] "Saved" is in the perfect tense.[5] The perfect tense indicates a past action with a present result. The passage could have been translated, in part, "…are being saved right now because of a past work of salvation…" The fact that it is in the indicative means that it is supposed to be the normal activity for believers to be saved in the present tense by grace through faith. It concerns God's present work of salvation in the believer's life, and the perfect tense of "saved" implies that it is ongoing because of a past action, that is the Cross.

It is not in the past tense of initial salvation. In other words, we are to live a life in Christ the same way that we were saved by Christ, by grace through faith. We are God's Workmanship in the present tense with very present results.[6]

If all of this sounds supernatural, it is.

> 12 Now we have received, not the spirit of the world, but the spirit which is of God; that we might know the things that are freely given to us of God. 13 Which things also we speak, not in the words which man's wisdom teacheth, but which the Holy Ghost teacheth; comparing spiritual things with spiritual. 14 But the natural man receiveth not the things of the Spirit of God: for they are foolishness unto him: neither can he know them, because they are spiritually discerned. 1 CORINTHIANS 2:12-14 (KJV)

It is sad, but all too often the Church today leads people to the Lord through simple faith only to require them to live a life of law thereafter. Other Churches that do not apply the law also do not apply the finished work of the Cross for a victorious Christian life. The result is lawlessness, no restraint, and inevitable sin.

THE ENEMIES WITHOUT

In the next several chapters, we will address the Spiritual Enemies that are most responsible for luring us out of fellowship with God: the Devil and his Satanic World System. These enemies are very real, but are seldom addressed today in the local Church.

CHAPTER THREE

OUR SPIRITUAL ENEMY–THE DEVIL

IN CHAPTER 2, WE LOOKED at the enemy within all men called the Flesh and discovered that the Holy Spirit, as a result of the Cross of Jesus Christ, is the only means of controlling the Flesh. In Chapter 3, we look at the history and power of the enemy without called the Devil, Satan, or Lucifer. Ironically, few people even acknowledge the Devil's existence, but he is very real and the Bible has much to say about him.

THE HISTORY OF THE DEVIL

The Devil is a created being whose primary job it was to guard the very throne of God. This is best seen in the lament of Ezekiel against the King of Tyrus, who is being told about Satan.

> *12 Son of man, take up a lamentation upon the king of Tyrus, and say unto him, Thus saith the Lord God; Thou sealest up the sum, full of wisdom, and perfect in beauty. 13 Thou hast been in Eden the garden of God; every precious stone was thy covering, the sardius, topaz, and the diamond, the beryl, the onyx, and the jasper, the sapphire, the emerald, and the carbuncle, and gold: the workmanship of thy tabrets and of thy pipes was prepared in thee in the day that thou wast created. 14 Thou art the anointed cherub that covereth; and I have set thee so:*

thou wast upon the holy mountain of God; thou hast walked up and down in the midst of the stones of fire. 15 Thou wast perfect in thy ways from the day that thou wast created, till iniquity was found in thee. 16 By the multitude of thy merchandise they have filled the midst of thee with violence, and thou hast sinned: therefore I will cast thee as profane out of the mountain of God: and I will destroy thee, O covering cherub, from the midst of the stones of fire. 17 Thine heart was lifted up because of thy beauty, thou hast corrupted thy wisdom by reason of thy brightness: I will cast thee to the ground, I will lay thee before kings, that they may behold thee. 18 Thou hast defiled thy sanctuaries by the multitude of thine iniquities, by the iniquity of thy traffick; therefore will I bring forth a fire from the midst of thee, it shall devour thee, and I will bring thee to ashes upon the earth in the sight of all them that behold thee. 19 All they that know thee among the people shall be astonished at thee: thou shalt be a terror, and never shalt thou be any more. EZEKIEL 28:12-19 (KJV)

This passage does not describe some ugly-looking creature in red with a pointed tail and a pitchfork. Instead we see a being that was "… full of wisdom, and perfect in beauty…" Satan was provided with every advantage that the Lord could give him, including access to the very throne of God. Satan's "iniquity" is described by Isaiah:

12 How art thou fallen from heaven, O Lucifer, son of the morning! how art thou cut down to the ground, which didst weaken the nations! 13 For thou hast said in thine heart, I will ascend into heaven, I will exalt my throne above the stars of God: I will sit also upon the mount of the congregation, in the sides of the north: 14 I will ascend above the heights of the clouds; I will be like the most High. 15 Yet thou shalt be brought down to hell, to the sides of the pit. ISAIAH 14:12-15 (KJV)

Satan's desire was to be "...like the most High..." As can be seen in the fall of man in Genesis 3:5, the Devil tried to export that idea to the Woman. Eve's temptation was to "...be as God knowing good and evil..." The strategy of the Devil is also his weakness; he is selfish as is evidenced by the seven "I will" statements found in the Isaiah passage.

There is a long-standing debate concerning the Devil's demise as to whether it happened in the past or if it is a future event. Both the Isaiah and Ezekiel passages present the demise of the Devil as a future event. The passage that discusses the actual Fall of Satan is written in the past tense.

> 7 And there was war in heaven: Michael and his angels fought against the dragon; and the dragon fought and his angels, 8 And prevailed not; neither was their place found any more in heaven. 9 And the great dragon was cast out, that old serpent, called the Devil, and Satan, which deceiveth the whole world: he was cast out into the earth, and his angels were cast out with him. REVELATION 12:7-9 (KJV)

This is a real battle, but when does it take place? In his classic book **Satan - His Motives and Methods**, Lewis Sperry Chafer provides some valuable insight.

> This is the first passage in the Word of God which declares Satan to be actually banished from Heaven. The passage also teaches that Satan remains in Heaven until the time herein described.
>
> According to the context it is that yet future time immediately preceding the setting up in the earth of the Kingdom of God and the power of His Christ.[1]

We see several other things in this passage including the fact that Satan has a host of angels with him who are defeated, so Satan is not alone. We also see that the spiritual battle in Heaven is going to be intense, yet the book of Jude gives us a glimpse into how the archangel Michael will fight it.

> 9 Yet Michael the archangel, when contending with the devil he disputed about the body of Moses, durst not bring against him a railing accusation, but said, The Lord rebuke thee. JUDE 9 (KJV)

The Devil is a mighty being, even among celestial beings. As a being created as the protector of the very throne of God, Satan has a place of prominence and the archangel Michael recognizes this fact. Michael does not fight in his own strength. As evidenced by his words, "…The Lord rebuke thee…," Michael demonstrates his total and true reliance upon the Lord. This is also a lesson for the Christian. If the mightiest of angels in Heaven must rely upon the Lord against the Devil, then we need not expect to be a match for him in our own strength.

THE SPHERE OF THE DEVIL

The book of Revelation also gives us some idea as to how far reaching the influence of the Devil really is. After the Devil is cast down at some future time, a statement is made as to what his position is today.

> 10 And I heard a loud voice saying in heaven, Now is come salvation, and strength, and the kingdom of our God, and the power of his Christ: for the accuser of our brethren is cast down, which accused them before our God day and night. REVELATION 12:10 (KJV)

Satan is the great accuser of the saints and he apparently makes every effort to affect our demise. If Satan is accusing the saints day and night, then there apparently is no moratorium on temptation. Satan also has access to the Earth and is free to come and go as he pleases. The temptation of Job makes this very clear.

6 Now there was a day when the sons of God came to present themselves before the Lord, and Satan came also among them.7 And the Lord said unto Satan, Whence comest thou? Then Satan answered the Lord, and said, From going to and fro in the earth, and from walking up and down in it. JOB 1:6-7 (KJV)

It is interesting to see that Satan is presented as one of the "sons of God" with access to the Lord Himself. The passage continues:

8 And the Lord said unto Satan, Hast thou considered my servant Job, that there is none like him in the earth, a perfect and an upright man, one that feareth God, and escheweth evil? 9 Then Satan answered the Lord, and said, Doth Job fear God for nought? 10 Hast not thou made an hedge about him, and about his house, and about all that he hath on every side? thou hast blessed the work of his hands, and his substance is increased in the land. 11 But put forth thine hand now, and touch all that he hath, and he will curse thee to thy face. 12 And the Lord said unto Satan, Behold, all that he hath is in thy power; only upon himself put not forth thine hand. So Satan went forth from the presence of the Lord. JOB 1:8-12 (KJV)

The activities of the Devil toward the saints are limited by God. The Devil can only do what the Lord allows him to do. Thus, Satan becomes a useful tool of the Lord in perfecting the believer. We have a promise of such limitation in the New Testament.

> *13 There hath no temptation taken you but such as is common to man: but God is faithful, who will not suffer you to be tempted above that ye are able; but will with the temptation also make a way to escape, that ye may be able to bear it. 1 CORINTHIANS 10:13 (KJV)*

This is very important. No matter what the temptation, we are without excuse for succumbing to it because God has promised that He will always make a way to overcome it. Therefore, God should not be blamed for our sin even though he has allowed the temptation.

The sphere of Satan extends far beyond the fact that he tempts the believer. This can be best seen in the temptation of our Lord and Savior.

> *5 And the devil, taking him up into an high mountain, shewed unto him all the kingdoms of the world in a moment of time. 6 And the devil said unto him, All this power will I give thee, and the glory of them: for that is delivered unto me; and to whomsoever I will I give it. 7 If thou therefore wilt worship me, all shall be thine. 8 And Jesus answered and said unto him, Get thee behind me, Satan: for it is written, Thou shalt worship the Lord thy God, and him only shalt thou serve. LUKE 4:5-8 (KJV)*

The temptations of Jesus will be reviewed more in depth, but this passage brings out an important fact about the Devil. The Devil gave Jesus images in His mind "in a moment of time," which indicates something about his methods. All of the kingdoms of the world are operated under his guidance and direction. It is truly a Satanic World System. As we look at worldly temptations, we will use that fact. In this case, the temptation was very shallow. He was asking the Lord and creator of Heaven and Earth to fall well below His position to worship an inferior created being. Yet as we will see Jesus was very much tempted as a man.

THE POWER OF THE DEVIL

The very world system that the Devil directs does not even believe that he exists, yet his power is stated in the book of Ephesians, albeit not that clearly.

> *1 And you hath he quickened, who were dead in trespasses and sins; 2 Wherein in time past ye walked according to the course of this world, according to the prince of the power of the air, the spirit that now worketh in the children of disobedience: 3 Among whom also we all had our conversation in times past in the lusts of our flesh, fulfilling the desires of the flesh and of the mind; and were by nature the children of wrath, even as others. EPHESIANS 2:1-3 (KJV)*

The ones who are quickened (made alive) are believers. The ones who are dead are those who have not believed unto salvation. These are also called "children of disobedience" and "children of wrath," and they are walking by some other means than the Spirit of God. They are said to walk in accordance with this world, but by means of "the prince of the power of the air," which is another name for the Devil. He is said to work in or energize[2] the unbeliever. This is similar to the work of the Holy Spirit in the life of the believer. If you have not been sealed with the Holy Spirit of promise, then you are basically nothing more than a puppet on a string for the Devil to do his bidding.

The power of Satan to energize the unsaved, control the Satanic World System, and to also be in Heaven accusing the saints continuously is more than some people are willing to accept, yet this is exactly what the Bible says about the Devil. Some attribute lesser powers to the Devil and say that he augments his abilities with his vast legions of fallen angels, and this is no doubt true to a great extent. Others say that the Devil has more important work than to worry about tempting individual believers. These people believe the Devil to be very finite in location and ability. The Bible, on the other hand, ascribes attributes to Satan that are far beyond anything that the human mind can imagine. Even giving a poor analogy has been impossible until recently, but the author will attempt to present this extremely poor analogy.

Consider the internet and its far-reaching capability. We now have the capability of putting a computer in every building in the world; not only every building, but several of them in every room in every building. These computers can be linked to every other computer via the internet. Voice and video conferencing capabilities exist for communications on the opposite side of the globe. We have physical limitations of speed, but for all practical purposes data transfer is nearly instantaneous. Now consider a super-computer that is tied into the internet with access to every other computer on the internet. At whim, this computer can access other computers, give them commands, and take historic data. Not only can it do this, but it has a protocol that allows it to do it with all other computers at the same time. Admittedly this is a poor analogy, but this may be something like the ability that God has given the Devil. To say that God could not do this is to say that the inventiveness of man is superior to that of God.

If this capability is not all that far-fetched in the physical realm (because it virtually exists today), then why would we discard similar or even greater capabilities in the spiritual realm? The Devil could be every bit as multi-tasking as any super-computer that we could imagine, yet our Lord and Savior is infinitely more powerful. As will be seen, there is some reason to believe that the Devil is finite in his abilities, but he is no doubt much more powerful than what most people give him credit for.

THE DEVIL AS A SPIRITUAL ENEMY

The Devil has two primary means of tempting the Christian. One is through his Satanic World System. These temptations will be dealt with in Chapter 4, but for now it should suffice to understand these temptations as resulting from physical things that we take in through our senses. Thus, worldly temptations are sensual in nature. Satan can also tempt us directly through our thoughts. When this occurs, we refer to this as the temptation of the Devil. Satan has a variety of means at his disposal to accomplish this task.

1. Wiles (Ephesians 6:11) – meaning crafty methods[3]

2. Devices (2 Corinthians 2:11) – meaning thoughts[4]

3. Snares (2 Timothy 2:26) – meaning lures and traps[5]

There are several places in the Scriptures where the believer is warned of the craftiness of the Devil, but the admonition is simply to recognize the temptations.

24 And the servant of the Lord must not strive; but be gentle unto all men, apt to teach, patient, 25 In meekness instructing those that oppose themselves; if God peradventure will give them repentance to the acknowledging of the truth; 26 And that they may recover themselves out of the snare of the devil, who are taken captive by him at his will. 2 TIMOTHY 2:24-26 (KJV)

There are several things in this passage that can assist the believer in understanding that a temptation is present. The first of these is the duty of the servant of the Lord to teach these things. Sadly, they are not taught today and most children of God find themselves in ignorance of the things of the Devil. The second thing is the most elemental part of repentance, an acknowledgement of the truth. This is because all Satanic temptations involve a lie in some form or another.

> *44 Ye are of your father the devil, and the lusts of your father ye will do. He was a murderer from the beginning, and abode not in the truth, because there is no truth in him. When he speaketh a lie, he speaketh of his own: for he is a liar, and the father of it. JOHN 8:44 (KJV)*

As will be seen, God provides the believer with assistance in recognizing the temptations of the Devil, but we are still admonished throughout Scripture to be sober and vigilant. The primary means of direct temptations by the Devil is through our thoughts.

> *11 Lest Satan should get an advantage of us: for we are not ignorant of his devices. 2 CORINTHIANS 2:11 (KJV)*

As previously mentioned, the term "devices" is the Greek word **noema** and actually means "thoughts." We are promised in this passage that we can know them when they are presented. If we know them, we can take the appropriate action that God lays out to deal with them. Satan's influence in controlling the thoughts of the believers and enticing them to sin is aptly described in the book of James.

> *13 Let no man say when he is tempted, I am tempted of God: for God cannot be tempted with evil, neither tempteth he any man: 14 But every man is tempted, when he is drawn away of his own lust, and enticed. 15 Then when lust hath conceived, it bringeth forth sin: and sin, when it is finished, bringeth forth death. JAMES 1:13-15 (KJV)*

The Devil presents the temptation and our sin nature is stirred to take over from there. At that point, the believer must make a choice and either follows the leading of the Holy Spirit or throws off the restraint of the Spirit and follows the leadings of their own flesh. If the believer recognizes the temptation and merely throws up their hands, realizing that they are no match for their flesh, the Holy Spirit will keep them from sin. If they do not recognize the temptation or try to handle it in their own strength through an external restrain of self-imposed law, the result will be sin and death.

GOD'S PURPOSE FOR TEMPTATIONS

When man fell in the Garden of Eden, he demonstrated his desire to live independently of God. This resulted in man's forced independence from God and broken fellowship with God because God is holy and just. Man, in his fallen state, is altogether sinful and wicked. At the Cross of Jesus Christ, several things occurred.

1. Jesus gave justice to God the Father by paying the sin debts for all mankind and for all time (1 John 2:2).

2. Our sin nature that we acquired as it was passed down from our father Adam was nailed to the Cross with our Lord (Romans 6:6).

3. The result of the Cross was regained fellowship and access to God (Ephesians 2:19).

4. Because of the finished work of Jesus on the Cross, we have received the Holy Spirit to help us (John 14:26).

5. This same Holy Spirit will keep us from sin (Galatians 5:16).

These things, and many more, God has provided for us in Jesus. What we lack is a desire to abandon our own independence and trust the Lord to keep us from sin. The Devil is thus our means of testing to encourage us to trust the Lord. Every temptation puts the believer at a crossroads of our own free will. We can choose to rely upon the Lord and allow Him to deliver us, or we can choose to manage our own problems without God and sin again.

Many believers make the mistake of thinking that the end goal of the Devil is to get us to do evil things. His own Satanic World System has many rules and regulations as an external restraint of law to encourage them not to sin. Satan's prize possession is not the drunken bum in the gutter. It is the person who lives independent of God. It should be no surprise that his temptations for Christians are designed to produce this as well. God, on the other hand, uses the divisiveness of the Devil to test and strengthen our faith through reliance on Him.

THE TEMPTATIONS OF THE DEVIL

What are these devices of the Devil that we need to be looking for? In his book **The Maturing Christian and His Enemies**, Warren Rushton suggests eleven types of temptations.[6] These temptations are defined separately, with two more added at the end.

PRIDE

This Satanic temptation is one that the Devil likes to employ against new believers:

> 6 Not a novice, lest being lifted up with pride he fall into the condemnation of the devil. 1 TIMOTHY 3:6 (KJV)

In this case, this statement is a warning concerning the appointment of elders. Pride is also associated with the Satanic World System, as we shall see in Chapter 4. Pride results from an attitude of superiority. Man, in his flesh, will always think himself to be smarter than God, and unfortunately, Christians fall into this trap as well. Satan plants the seeds of pride to take us out of fellowship with God, thereby hindering our spirituality and our witness for the Lord.

AGE CONFORMING

This temptation may be tied closely with the temptations of the world and depends on how the temptation is presented.

> *3 But if our gospel be hid, it is hid to them that are lost: 4 In whom the god of this world hath blinded the minds of them which believe not, lest the light of the glorious gospel of Christ, who is the image of God, should shine unto them. 2 CORINTHIANS 4:3-4 (KJV)*

In this passage, the term used for the Devil is "god of this world" (better translated "god of this age"), and it is apparent that the Devil conforms the unbelieving to his own message rather than the message of the Cross. Thus "age conforming" is to act in a manner that is independent of God and looks like the world (or is of this age). Christians are not immune to this, and the temptation for ministries to be worldly runs rampant. But such is not the admonition of the Lord.

> *2 And be not conformed to this world: but be ye transformed by the renewing of your mind, that ye may prove what is that good, and acceptable, and perfect, will of God. 3 For I say, through the grace given unto me, to every man that is among you, not to think of himself more highly than he ought to think; but to think soberly, according as God hath dealt to every man the measure of faith. ROMANS 12:2-3 (KJV)*

The term for "world" is **aion,** and it means "age".[7] The phrase "be not conformed to this age" could easily be translated "be not secular" or "stop being secular." For some reason secularism is something that most Christians consider to be neutral towards God, but it is actually independence from God. By disguising the intent, the Devil seeks to neutralize our relationship with the Lord. More will be said about this in Chapter 5.

WORRY

Seldom does anyone associate worry with the Devil, but we see this very clearly from Scripture.

> 7 Casting all your care upon him; for he careth for you. 8 Be sober, be vigilant; because your adversary the devil, as a roaring lion, walketh about, seeking whom he may devour: 9 Whom resist stedfast in the faith, knowing that the same afflictions are accomplished in your brethren that are in the world. 1 PETER 5:7-9 (KJV)

Worry normally results from a desire to control or change something that is not under our control. Therefore we are to cast these things upon the Lord and resign ourselves to His sovereignty, knowing that He will do what is best for us. We are also fortunate to have a promise that goes with the warning.

> 10 But the God of all grace, who hath called us unto his eternal glory by Christ Jesus, after that ye have suffered a while, make you perfect, stablish, strengthen, settle you. 1 PETER 5:10 (KJV)

The Devil will use worry to try to deceive us into acting independently of God and not trusting Him. The description of the Devil eating us as a lion is all too appropriate. Worry can lead to our next temptation, discouragement, and may result in depression.

DISCOURAGEMENT

Discouragement is something that often leads to depression. The remedy of the world for this is to take some pills to overcome it. Unfortunately, like its cousin worry, few people will recognize discouragement as a Satanic temptation. The classical account of the temptation of discouragement is the temptation of Job.

> *6 Now there was a day when the sons of God came to present themselves before the Lord, and Satan came also among them. 7 And the Lord said unto Satan, Whence comest thou? Then Satan answered the Lord, and said, From going to and fro in the earth, and from walking up and down in it. 8 And the Lord said unto Satan, Hast thou considered my servant Job, that there is none like him in the earth, a perfect and an upright man, one that feareth God, and escheweth evil? 9 Then Satan answered the Lord, and said, Doth Job fear God for nought? 10 Hast not thou made an hedge about him, and about his house, and about all that he hath on every side? thou hast blessed the work of his hands, and his substance is increased in the land. 11 But put forth thine hand now, and touch all that he hath, and he will curse thee to thy face. 12 And the Lord said unto Satan, Behold, all that he hath is in thy power; only upon himself put not forth thine hand. So Satan went forth from the presence of the Lord. JOB 1:6-12 (KJV)*

This is a good place to stop and remind ourselves that the Devil is limited by God in his ability to tempt the believer. I am not sure that Job saw it that way at the time, but we have precious promises previously mentioned to back this up. The first temptation of Job continues.

13 And there was a day when his sons and his daughters were eating and drinking wine in their eldest brother's house: 14 And there came a messenger unto Job, and said, The oxen were plowing, and the asses feeding beside them: 15 And the Sabeans fell upon them, and took them away; yea, they have slain the servants with the edge of the sword; and I only am escaped alone to tell thee. 16 While he was yet speaking, there came also another, and said, The fire of God is fallen from heaven, and hath burned up the sheep, and the servants, and consumed them; and I only am escaped alone to tell thee. 17 While he was yet speaking, there came also another, and said, The Chaldeans made out three bands, and fell upon the camels, and have carried them away, yea, and slain the servants with the edge of the sword; and I only am escaped alone to tell thee. 18 While he was yet speaking, there came also another, and said, Thy sons and thy daughters were eating and drinking wine in their eldest brother's house: 19 And, behold, there came a great wind from the wilderness, and smote the four corners of the house, and it fell upon the young men, and they are dead; and I only am escaped alone to tell thee. 20 Then Job arose, and rent his mantle, and shaved his head, and fell down upon the ground, and worshipped, 21 And said, Naked came I out of my mother's womb, and naked shall I return thither: the Lord gave, and the Lord hath taken away; blessed be the name of the Lord. 22 In all this Job sinned not, nor charged God foolishly. JOB 1:13-22 (KJV)

Job was very sad after the Devil had used the resources from his Satanic World System to work him over, but his faith in God did not waver. The first attempt by the Devil was unsuccessful, so the Lord let Satan try again.

1 Again there was a day when the sons of God came to present themselves before the Lord, and Satan came also among them to present himself before the Lord. 2 And the Lord said unto Satan, From whence comest thou? And Satan answered the Lord, and said, From going to and fro in the earth, and from walking up and down in it. 3 And the Lord said unto Satan, Hast thou considered my servant Job, that there is none like him in the earth, a perfect and an upright man, one that feareth God, and escheweth evil? and still he holdeth fast his integrity, although thou movedst me against him, to destroy him without cause. 4 And Satan answered the Lord, and said, Skin for skin, yea, all that a man hath will he give for his life. 5 But put forth thine hand now, and touch his bone and his flesh, and he will curse thee to thy face. 6 And the Lord said unto Satan, Behold, he is in thine hand; but save his life. JOB 2:1-6 (KJV)

Once again Satan had to ask permission to harm Job, but this time we see something new in the Devil's arsenal. The Devil assails Job with a physical affliction.

7 So went Satan forth from the presence of the Lord, and smote Job with sore boils from the sole of his foot unto his crown. 8 And he took him a potsherd to scrape himself withal; and he sat down among the ashes. 9 Then said his wife unto him, Dost thou still retain thine integrity? curse God, and die. 10 But he said unto her, Thou speakest as one of the foolish women speaketh. What? shall we receive good at the hand of God, and shall we not receive evil? In all this did not Job sin with his lips. JOB 2:7-10 (KJV)

Others around us can be both a curse and a blessing. In this case, Job's wife was an added source of discouragement, but it says that Job did not sin. It is not as apparent that Job is caving into the Devil until you read on and see passages such as:

11 Why died I not from the womb? why did I not give up the ghost when I came out of the belly? JOB 3:11 (KJV)

Obviously, the Devil was the real source of Job's discouragement, but he did not realize this fact. And so it is with most Christians who find themselves discouraged by circumstances which may or may not be within their control. As with worry, trusting the Lord is all important when dealing with discouragement and depression. Care should be taken not to trust drugs to overcome discouragement. You often substitute one problem for another. It also helps to have good friends who can encourage you rather than the friends of Job who blamed him for his ills, telling him that it was the just punishment of God. We do reap what we sow and we need to repent of our sins, but it is the job of the believer to help restore a relationship with the Lord and with others. It is not the job of the believer to be judge, jury, and executioner concerning the circumstances of others.

COWARDICE IN SPIRITUAL THINGS

There are several worldly sources for cowardice in spiritual things. Some of this arises from confusion in Christian circles regarding just what our spiritual responsibilities are. The Apostle Peter is a good example of this. At the last supper, Jesus told Peter that he would be under the attack of the Devil.

31 And the Lord said, Simon, Simon, behold, Satan hath desired to have you, that he may sift you as wheat: 32 But I have prayed for thee, that thy faith fail not: and when thou art converted, strengthen thy brethren. 33 And he said unto him, Lord, I am ready to go with thee, both into prison, and to death. 34 And he said, I tell thee, Peter, the cock shall not crow this day, before that thou shalt thrice deny that thou knowest me. LUKE 22:31-34 (KJV)

Later when Jesus was confronted in the Garden of Gethsemane, Peter cut off the ear of the High Priest's servant, and Jesus immediately stopped the altercation, even healing the ear (Luke 22:47-53). No doubt Peter was confused and perplexed by this action especially after hearing what Jesus had to say at the last supper immediately after telling him that he was going to be tempted.

> 35 And he said unto them, When I sent you without purse, and scrip, and shoes, lacked ye any thing? And they said, Nothing. 36 Then said he unto them, But now, he that hath a purse, let him take it, and likewise his scrip: and he that hath no sword, let him sell his garment, and buy one. 37 For I say unto you, that this that is written must yet be accomplished in me, And he was reckoned among the transgressors: for the things concerning me have an end. 38 And they said, Lord, behold, here are two swords. And he said unto them, It is enough. LUKE 22:35-38 (KJV)

Not understanding the plan of God, Peter only understood his spiritual battle in physical terms. Being told to get a sword and then using a sword to defend the Lord must have seemed logical to Peter. Being rebuked of the Lord for using the sword obviously left him hurt and confused. This left him as ripe pickings for the Devil.

> 54 Then took they him, and led him, and brought him into the high priest's house. And Peter followed afar off. 55 And when they had kindled a fire in the midst of the hall, and were set down together, Peter sat down among them. 56 But a certain maid beheld him as he sat by the fire, and earnestly looked upon him, and said, This man was also with him. 57 And he denied him, saying, Woman, I know him not. 58 And after a little while another saw him, and said, Thou art also of them. And Peter said, Man, I am not. 59 And about the space of one hour after

another confidently affirmed, saying, Of a truth this fellow also was with him: for he is a Galilaean. 60 And Peter said, Man, I know not what thou sayest. And immediately, while he yet spake, the cock crew. 61 And the Lord turned, and looked upon Peter. And Peter remembered the word of the Lord, how he had said unto him, Before the cock crow, thou shalt deny me thrice. 62 And Peter went out, and wept bitterly. LUKE 22:54-62 (KJV)

There are many Christians in our day who truly desire to serve the Lord but are confused by the worldly trappings of the modern Church. Many of these trappings have led to sin among the brethren because they have nothing to do with the simple message of the Cross of Jesus Christ. The confusion in the message often leaves Christians open and vulnerable to temptation. More will be said about the worldly trappings of the modern Church in Part 2.

Another source of "Spiritual Cowardice" is embarrassment, which leads to a lack of boldness. The Apostle Paul recognized his own struggle in this regard. Immediately following the passage on the Armor of God is an admonishment to pray for the saints. Paul then continues this prayer for himself.

19 And for me, that utterance may be given unto me, that I may open my mouth boldly, to make known the mystery of the gospel, 20 For which I am an ambassador in bonds: that therein I may speak boldly, as I ought to speak. EPHESIANS 6:19-20 (KJV)

The obvious proximity to the Armor of God demonstrates that the Apostle Paul understood that cowardice in spiritual things is a Satanic temptation. In a day and age when we are restricted with "separation of church and state" and "secular world verses Christianity," Christians are often intimidated into silence concerning their faith. This is of the Devil, and we should pray as Paul did for boldness in our faith.

STEALING

Stealing is something that most people would consider to be a temptation from the Devil, since theft of faith is attributed to him in the parable of the sower and the seed.

> 12 Those by the way side are they that hear; then cometh the devil, and taketh away the word out of their hearts, lest they should believe and be saved. LUKE 8:12 (KJV)

It is therefore no surprise that the Devil tempts believers to steal.

> 27 Neither give place to the devil. 28 Let him that stole steal no more: but rather let him labour, working with his hands the thing which is good, that he may have to give to him that needeth. EPHESIANS 4:27-28 (KJV)

There are many self-justifications for stealing and the Devil will use them all to encourage the Believer to break fellowship with God. This passage is more of an admonishment to stop sinning than it is to not sin in the first place. So, it is with most of us and it is not limited to just stealing.

LYING

Lying is the Devil's hallmark, as has been previously stated.

> 44 Ye are of your father the devil, and the lusts of your father ye will do. He was a murderer from the beginning, and abode not in the truth, because there is no truth in him. When he speaketh a lie, he speaketh of his own: for he is a liar, and the father of it. JOHN 8:42 (KJV)

Revelation 20:8,10 also says that the Devil deceives the nations. The classical account of lying and its consequences is found in the book of Acts with the account of Ananias and Sapphira.

5 But a certain man named Ananias, with Sapphira his wife, sold a possession, 2 And kept back part of the price, his wife also being privy to it, and brought a certain part, and laid it at the apostles' feet. 3 But Peter said, Ananias, why hath Satan filled thine heart to lie to the Holy Ghost, and to keep back part of the price of the land? 4 Whiles it remained, was it not thine own? and after it was sold, was it not in thine own power? why hast thou conceived this thing in thine heart? thou hast not lied unto men, but unto God. 5 And Ananias hearing these words fell down, and gave up the ghost: and great fear came on all them that heard these things. 6 And the young men arose, wound him up, and carried him out, and buried him. 7 And it was about the space of three hours after, when his wife, not knowing what was done, came in. 8 And Peter answered unto her, Tell me whether ye sold the land for so much? And she said, Yea, for so much. 9 Then Peter said unto her, How is it that ye have agreed together to tempt the Spirit of the Lord? behold, the feet of them which have buried thy husband are at the door, and shall carry thee out. 10 Then fell she down straightway at his feet, and yielded up the ghost: and the young men came in, and found her dead, and, carrying her forth, buried her by her husband. ACTS 5:1-10 (KJV)

The Apostle Peter identifies Ananias' lying as a Satanic temptation in verse 3. The harsh consequences are a clear indication of God's displeasure with lying and His impatience with it. The truth about our sin is essential for God's forgiveness and it distinguishes the believing from the unbelieving.

19 And this is the condemnation, that light is come into the world, and men loved darkness rather than light, because their deeds were evil. 20 For every one that doeth evil hateth the light, neither cometh to the light, lest his deeds should be reproved. 21 But he that doeth truth cometh to the light, that his deeds may be made manifest, that they are wrought in God. JOHN 3:19-21 (KJV)

LAZINESS IN SPIRITUAL THINGS, TALE BEARING, AND BUSYBODY

These three temptations are all found in the same location in Scripture and they are usually associated with idleness.

11 But the younger widows refuse: for when they have begun to wax wanton against Christ, they will marry; 12 Having damnation, because they have cast off their first faith. 13 And withal they learn to be idle, wandering about from house to house; and not only idle, but tattlers also and busybodies, speaking things which they ought not. 14 I will therefore that the younger women marry, bear children, guide the house, give none occasion to the adversary to speak reproachfully. 15 For some are already turned aside after Satan. 1 TIMOTHY 5:11-15 (KJV)

The admonishment here is toward young widows, but it could just as easily apply to "praying more intelligently" on a prayer chain regardless of age, gender, or marital status. Idleness leads to curiosity and gossip. It is better to mind one's own business rather than to spread rumors spawned from inaccurate or contrived knowledge. Even if the tale is related from the truth, the mission of the Church, to be reconciled to God and one another, could be compromised. In this case, the "adversary" is the Devil who comes before the Lord accusing the Saints day and night. As is clear from verse 15, when believers meddle and gossip they are falling into temptation and doing the Devil's bidding.

AN UNFORGIVING SPIRIT

I remember being told that forgiveness is something that you must do because if you did not then God would exclude you from Heaven. I was also told that forgiveness is one sided irrespective of whether the person wants to be forgiven and that its purpose is to make me feel better. I noticed that many people gravitated towards this unilateral forgiveness because they wanted to avoid the confrontation required for reconciliation. After studying forgiveness in the Scriptures, I realized that the means, purpose, and mechanism have all been distorted into something that the Bible never intended. This can best be seen in studying God's forgiveness.

> 9 If we confess our sins, he is faithful and just to forgive us our sins, and to cleanse us from all unrighteousness. 1 JOHN 1:9 (KJV)

Notice first that forgiveness with God is not unconditional; it requires confession, or agreement with God, that we have sinned. We must recognize our sinful condition and tell the truth about our sins. This means that God's forgiveness is not unilateral (one sided). We must want to be forgiven. If this were not the case, then everyone would be forgiven, everyone would be going to Heaven, and Hell would be an empty, lonely place. We know that this is not the case as Revelation 20 and 21 tell us how God will judge the world. We also do not see anything in the Scriptures about God forgiving man to make Himself feel better. It is clear from Scripture that the purpose of forgiveness is reconciliation and renewed fellowship with God.

So how does this relate to forgiveness among men?

32 And be ye kind one to another, tenderhearted, forgiving one another, even as God for Christ's sake hath forgiven you. EPHESIANS 4:32 (KJV)

If we are to forgive others in the same way that "…God for Christ's sake hath forgiven you…," then it should be for the same purpose and by the same means. It should be based upon the truth and for restoring relationships. Notice that the Ephesians passage talks about our attitude, but it does not attribute feeling better to forgiveness. In fact, I could not find any statements like that in the entire Bible. Admittedly many will disagree, but it is hard to escape the teachings of Scripture on the subject. It is apparently impossible to forgive someone who does not want to be forgiven; nor can we expect forgiveness from someone who does not want to give it, even if we apologize.

The word "forgive" in Scripture means to "send away" or to "let go of."[8] This is similar to the idea of casting our cares upon the Lord (1 Peter 5:7-9). Therefore, being relieved of the responsibility for holding onto something because of the inaction of another is available to the believer. Unfortunately, the god of this world has lied to modify both the definition and purpose of forgiveness.

From a Biblical perspective, what does it mean not to forgive? It obviously goes deeper than a unilateral mental dismissing of damage. It also requires more than an acknowledgement of an apology. Forgiveness requires a willingness to reconcile after being hurt or damaged. This is much more difficult than the intellectual assent required in unilateral forgiveness as defined by the world. It requires the one forgiving to open themselves to receive more damage. That is why the truth and repentance are so important. The Devil has corrupted this requirement among believers.

10 To whom ye forgive any thing, I forgive also: for if I forgave any thing,
to whom I forgave it, for your sakes forgave I it in the person of Christ;
11 Lest Satan should get an advantage of us: for we are not ignorant of
his devices. 2 CORINTHIANS 2:10-11 (KJV)

Notice that the Apostle Paul conditioned his forgiveness on the forgiveness provided by the Corinthian Church. This passage may have been written in regard to a repentant fornicator described in 1 Corinthians 5. Paul had admonished the Corinthian Church to isolate and exclude this individual. Reconciliation on the part of the Church would be required upon repentance. Since our sin nature likes to hold grudges, Paul's admonition to forgive was probably required. Paul made a more direct appeal to the Galatian Church.

1 Brethren, if a man be overtaken in a fault, ye which are spiritual,
restore such an one in the spirit of meekness; considering thyself, lest
thou also be tempted. GALATIANS 6:1 (KJV)

Here again the temptation would be to be unforgiving because of self-righteousness. More than that it is a temptation not to reconcile and restore relationships. God is our example in this.

18 And all things are of God, who hath reconciled us to himself by Jesus
Christ, and hath given to us the ministry of reconciliation; 19 To wit,
that God was in Christ, reconciling the world unto himself, not imputing
their trespasses unto them; and hath committed unto us the word of
reconciliation. 2 CORINTHIANS 5:18-19 (KJV)

This ministry of reconciliation God has given to us:

20 Now then we are ambassadors for Christ, as though God did beseech you by us: we pray you in Christ's stead, be ye reconciled to God. 2 CORINTHIANS 5:20 (KJV)

Sadly, the Church is losing any sense of reconciliation because of poor doctrine. If we cannot reconcile one another, we will hardly be ministers reconciling men to God. Without reconciliation as the goal, forgiveness is impossible.

INDECISION

Since the Devil has access to our thoughts, planting indecision should be no surprise.

5 If any of you lack wisdom, let him ask of God, that giveth to all men liberally, and upbraideth not; and it shall be given him. 6 But let him ask in faith, nothing wavering. For he that wavereth is like a wave of the sea driven with the wind and tossed. 7 For let not that man think that he shall receive any thing of the Lord. 8 A double minded man is unstable in all his ways. JAMES 1:5-8 (KJV)

Many people have trouble making up their mind, but few attribute that to the Devil.

7 Submit yourselves therefore to God. Resist the devil, and he will flee from you. 8 Draw nigh to God, and he will draw nigh to you. Cleanse your hands, ye sinners; and purify your hearts, ye double minded. JAMES 4:7-8 (KJV)

The fact that the individual has an impure heart gives way for the Devil to plant indecision. The indecision in turn creates instability, and the result is inaction. The James 1 passage pinpoints the problem as a lack of trust in God's leading that the Devil can take advantage of.

BETRAYAL OF THE FAITHFUL

Throughout history, the faithful of God have faced persecution and all manner of trials. The book of Hebrews gives us some profound examples.

> *32 And what shall I more say? for the time would fail me to tell of Gedeon, and of Barak, and of Samson, and of Jephthae; of David also, and Samuel, and of the prophets: 33 Who through faith subdued kingdoms, wrought righteousness, obtained promises, stopped the mouths of lions, 34 Quenched the violence of fire, escaped the edge of the sword, out of weakness were made strong, waxed valiant in fight, turned to flight the armies of the aliens. 35 Women received their dead raised to life again: and others were tortured, not accepting deliverance; that they might obtain a better resurrection: 36 And others had trial of cruel mockings and scourgings, yea, moreover of bonds and imprisonment: 37 They were stoned, they were sawn asunder, were tempted, were slain with the sword: they wandered about in sheepskins and goatskins; being destitute, afflicted, tormented; 38 (Of whom the world was not worthy:) they wandered in deserts, and in mountains, and in dens and caves of the earth. HEBREWS 11:32-38 (KJV)*

We see trials for the Church throughout history, including imprisonment, torture, crucifixion, burning, and all manner of cruel behavior. In the betrayal of our Lord, we find that Satan was behind it all.

> *3 Then entered Satan into Judas surnamed Iscariot, being of the number of the twelve. 4 And he went his way, and communed with the chief priests and captains, how he might betray him unto them. LUKE 22:3 (KJV)*

Judas betrayed the Lord for money.

14 Then one of the twelve, called Judas Iscariot, went unto the chief priests, 15 And said unto them, What will ye give me, and I will deliver him unto you? And they covenanted with him for thirty pieces of silver. 16 And from that time he sought opportunity to betray him. MATTHEW 26:14-16 (KJV)

When the time came for the betrayal Judas had already succumb to the temptation.

2 And supper being ended, the devil having now put into the heart of Judas Iscariot, Simon's son, to betray him; JOHN 13:2 (KJV)

Judas must have been very cold of heart, betraying the Lord in an act of friendship.

47 And while he yet spake, behold a multitude, and he that was called Judas, one of the twelve, went before them, and drew near unto Jesus to kiss him. 48 But Jesus said unto him, Judas, betrayest thou the Son of man with a kiss? LUKE 22:47-48 (KJV)

Once Judas figured out the consequences of his actions, he eventually took his own life in regret. There is no indication in Scripture that Judas realized the source of his temptation as being the Devil.

There are many well-meaning people, Christians included, who have betrayed believers who practice their faith in God. Many refuse to put their children in the Atheistic Government Schools, preferring a Godlier education at home or in a Christian school. Quite often their own churches turn them into the local authorities. Others who spank their children are even turned in to Government Social Services by their pastors. Families have been laid waste by well-meaning Christian busybodies who think Government, and not the family, are to care for children and the elderly.

Many misguided believers hold the same view as the nineteenth-century German philosopher, Georg Wilhelm Friedrich Hegel, that Government is God walking upon the Earth. These are the same ideas that eventually led to Adolph Hitler, the Nazi Party, and the rise of the Third Reich. Many Germans considered themselves to be Christians and the Jews to be "Christ Killers." It is chilling how easy it was to manipulate the so-called Christian community into accepting Hitler. Here again, the Devil was most likely in the details and many Jews and Christians were betrayed.

THE DEFENSE AGAINST THE DEVIL

As with all spiritual warfare, our defenses against this spiritual enemy are not natural. They are supernatural. We would have no chance whatsoever on our own to defeat this angelic being who possesses such great power both in Heaven and on Earth. What we have is what God provides and it is all sufficient.

> *3 For though we walk in the flesh, we do not war after the flesh: 4 (For the weapons of our warfare are not carnal, but mighty through God to the pulling down of strong holds;) 5 Casting down imaginations, and every high thing that exalteth itself against the knowledge of God, and bringing into captivity every thought to the obedience of Christ;*
> *2 CORINTHIANS 10:3-5 (KJV)*

This fact is emphasized again when our defenses against Satanic attack are introduced.

10 Finally, my brethren, be strong in the Lord, and in the power of his might. 11 Put on the whole armour of God, that ye may be able to stand against the wiles of the devil. 12 For we wrestle not against flesh and blood, but against principalities, against powers, against the rulers of the darkness of this world, against spiritual wickedness in high places. 13 Wherefore take unto you the whole armour of God, that ye may be able to withstand in the evil day, and having done all, to stand.
EPHESIANS 6:10-13 (KJV)

We are never admonished to be strong in ourselves. We are to be "… strong in the Lord, and in the power of His might…" We cannot battle an enemy that we cannot see and of whom it is written that the Archangel Michael would not speak out against (Jude 9). Our power is in the Lord and He alone can deliver us. What He has delivered to us is a protective armor that allows us to stand and withstand the Devil's temptations. We are not to go on the offensive. We are merely to stand and resist.

7 Submit yourselves therefore to God. Resist the devil, and he will flee from you. 8 Draw nigh to God, and he will draw nigh to you. Cleanse your hands, ye sinners; and purify your hearts, ye double minded.
JAMES 4:7-8 (KJV)

Even though the Armor of God is spiritual in nature, it is also very practical. When many Christians look at it they fail to realize what it is and how it is used. It is surprising how many Christians do not even believe that they are tempted of the Devil. They believe that the deceiver is so finite as to make it impossible for him to tempt anyone because they do not believe he can be so many places at one time. If this were the case then the Apostle Paul wasted a great deal of time and effort in warning us about the Devil. Read below what the Apostle Paul writes about our defense against the Devil.

> *14 Stand therefore, having your loins girt about with truth, and having on the breastplate of righteousness; 15 And your feet shod with the preparation of the gospel of peace; 16 Above all, taking the shield of faith, wherewith ye shall be able to quench all the fiery darts of the wicked. 17 And take the helmet of salvation, and the sword of the Spirit, which is the word of God: EPHESIANS 6:14-17 (KJV)*

There are six pieces of armor, all of them supplied by the Lord, and all of them with a very practical purpose.

TRUTH

It is very common for the Girdle of Truth to be mistaken for the Word of God. We know that it is not because we have the Sword of the Spirit for this. Truth is the first piece of armor because the Devil is a liar and a deceiver as has already been stated. As armor supplied by God, the Girdle of Truth is a God given ability to distinguish the truth from a lie. It is the ability to see things as they really are as opposed to the way the Devil presents them. The Apostle Peter obviously exercised this ability when he confronted Ananias and Sapphira (Acts 5:1-10). This piece of armor is very key because it is the point at which any temptation of the Devil is recognized. The Devil hinders the lost from seeing the truth perpetually.

> *3 But if our gospel be hid, it is hid to them that are lost: 4 In whom the god of this world hath blinded the minds of them which believe not, lest the light of the glorious gospel of Christ, who is the image of God, should shine unto them. 2 CORINTHIANS 4:3-4 (KJV)*

Believers, on the other hand, are enlightened by God.

27 But God hath chosen the foolish things of the world to confound the wise; and God hath chosen the weak things of the world to confound the things which are mighty; 28 And base things of the world, and things which are despised, hath God chosen, yea, and things which are not, to bring to nought things that are: 29 That no flesh should glory in his presence. 30 But of him are ye in Christ Jesus, who of God is made unto us wisdom, and righteousness, and sanctification, and redemption: 31 That, according as it is written, He that glorieth, let him glory in the Lord. 1 CORINTHIANS 1:27-31 (KJV)

Believers can take no credit for the ability to see truth and how it has been distorted by the Devil into a lie. It is a resource supplied by God.

RIGHTEOUSNESS

The Breastplate of Righteousness can only be supplied by God. We have no righteousness of our own.

25 Whom God hath set forth to be a propitiation through faith in his blood, to declare his righteousness for the remission of sins that are past, through the forbearance of God; 26 To declare, I say, at this time his righteousness: that he might be just, and the justifier of him which believeth in Jesus. 27 Where is boasting then? It is excluded. By what law? of works? Nay: but by the law of faith. ROMANS 3:25-27 (KJV)

It is good to remember that positionally Christ is all our righteousness. As a practical matter, the Breastplate of Righteousness goes beyond the acknowledgment of position. Christ, being our righteousness and the justifier of the saints, will always supply and make evident a right course of action that is pleasing to God. The Lord will never lead us into sin. Even if the right thing is the most difficult, most expensive, least likely to succeed in the Flesh, or most embarrassing, the Lord will provide the method and the means to accomplish His will. The right thing to do will be right in substance and in motive. This again is supernatural and relies totally on the Lord. Such reliance on God is not something that is peculiar to the New Testament. King Solomon saw it in his day.

> 5 Trust in the Lord with all thine heart; and lean not unto thine own understanding. 6 In all thy ways acknowledge him, and he shall direct thy paths. 7 Be not wise in thine own eyes: fear the Lord, and depart from evil. PROVERBS 3:5-7 (KJV)

PREPARATION OF THE GOSPEL OF PEACE

It may be true that many people feel better when they are telling others about the Lord, but that is probably not what the "Preparation of the Gospel of Peace" is talking about. The ability to appropriate the Armor of God presupposes that the individual is walking by the Holy Spirit.

> 1 There is therefore now no condemnation to them which are in Christ Jesus, who walk not after the flesh, but after the Spirit. 2 For the law of the Spirit of life in Christ Jesus hath made me free from the law of sin and death. ROMANS 8:1-2 (KJV)

Therefore the "Preparation of the Gospel of Peace" is the fact that the individual meets the temptation in fellowship with God and walking by means of the Holy Spirit. The present work of salvation in the believer's life is our Good News for today. We have peace with God because we are in fellowship with God, and God is our ever-present refuge in times of temptation. We cannot overcome sin on our own.

FAITH

The Shield of Faith to stop the Devil's arrows of fire is an open and direct reference to trusting in God to deal with any situation. There is nothing that surprises the Lord because He is all knowing. There is nothing too immense for the Lord because He is all powerful. Trusting the Lord should have no risk because by faith we know that He is always in control when we let Him be.

28 And we know that all things work together for good to them that love God, to them who are the called according to his purpose. ROMANS 8:28 (KJV)

We also have a promise from God that He will only allow temptations from the Devil that we are able to handle.

13 There hath no temptation taken you but such as is common to man: but God is faithful, who will not suffer you to be tempted above that ye are able; but will with the temptation also make a way to escape, that ye may be able to bear it. 1 CORINTHIANS 10:13 (KJV)

No matter what the Devil wants to do, he is limited by God. Our way of escape includes trusting the Lord for the answers and having faith that He is always in control. We see that this faith must be able to deal with the Devil's devices.

16 Above all, taking the shield of faith, wherewith ye shall be able to quench all the fiery darts of the wicked. EPHESIANS 6:16 (KJV)

These fiery darts would include worry, depression, pride, or any other device of the Devil we have already looked at.

SALVATION

The Helmet of Salvation protecting the head intimates the knowledge that we have that we are saved past, present, and future. This is not only positionally true, but it is practically true as well. Most of Romans 8 is dedicated to our present deliverance by God. More is said in Chapter 7 about the rich truth concerning our present salvation. It is important to remember that WHAT we are saved from is sin. The temptations of the Devil try to pull us out of fellowship with God so that we WILL sin, but our new relationship with God can keep us FROM sin. An excerpt is given from Romans 8 in this regard.

2 For the law of the Spirit of life in Christ Jesus hath made me free from the law of sin and death. 3 For what the law could not do, in that it was weak through the flesh, God sending his own Son in the likeness of sinful flesh, and for sin, condemned sin in the flesh: 4 That the righteousness of the law might be fulfilled in us, who walk not after the flesh, but after the Spirit. 5 For they that are after the flesh do mind the things of the flesh; but they that are after the Spirit the things of the Spirit. 6 For to be carnally minded is death; but to be spiritually minded is life and peace. 7 Because the carnal mind is enmity against God: for it is not subject to the law of God, neither indeed can be. 8 So then they that are in the flesh cannot please God. 9 But ye are not in the flesh, but in the Spirit, if so be that the Spirit of God dwell in you. Now if any man have not the Spirit of Christ, he is none of his. 10 And if Christ be in you, the body is dead because of sin; but the Spirit is life because of righteousness. 11 But if the Spirit of him that raised up Jesus from the dead dwell in you, he that raised up Christ from the dead shall also quicken your mortal bodies by his Spirit that dwelleth in you. 12 Therefore, brethren, we are debtors, not to the flesh, to live after the flesh. 13 For if ye live after the flesh,

ye shall die: but if ye through the Spirit do mortify the deeds of the
body, ye shall live. ROMANS 8:2-13 (KJV)

The key to God's present work of salvation in each of us is our relationship to Him through the Cross of Jesus Christ. Though it is completely supernatural in that it does not even rest in something tangible for us to grasp, it is very practical indeed.

WORD OF GOD

"...The Sword of the Spirit, which is the Word of God...," is the one piece of armor that is physical in nature. Even so, it is given by God. The Word of God has several purposes, not the least of which is to give us insight into the character and expectations of God. Walking by the Holy Spirit is what He expects us to do, but sinning is what He expects us not to do.

16 All scripture is given by inspiration of God, and is profitable for
doctrine, for reproof, for correction, for instruction in righteousness:
17 That the man of God may be perfect, throughly furnished unto all
good works. 2 TIMOTHY 3:16-17 (KJV)

It could be argued that as a "Sword," the Word of God should be a defensive weapon, but this is not how the Lord used it.

1 And Jesus being full of the Holy Ghost returned from Jordan, and was
led by the Spirit into the wilderness, 2 Being forty days tempted of the
devil. And in those days he did eat nothing: and when they were ended,
he afterward hungered. 3 And the devil said unto him, If thou be the
Son of God, command this stone that it be made bread. 4 And Jesus
answered him, saying, It is written, That man shall not live by bread
alone, but by every word of God. 5 And the devil, taking him up into

an high mountain, shewed unto him all the kingdoms of the world in a moment of time. 6 And the devil said unto him, All this power will I give thee, and the glory of them: for that is delivered unto me; and to whomsoever I will I give it. 7 If thou therefore wilt worship me, all shall be thine. 8 And Jesus answered and said unto him, Get thee behind me, Satan: for it is written, Thou shalt worship the Lord thy God, and him only shalt thou serve. 9 And he brought him to Jerusalem, and set him on a pinnacle of the temple, and said unto him, If thou be the Son of God, cast thyself down from hence: 10 For it is written, He shall give his angels charge over thee, to keep thee: 11 And in their hands they shall bear thee up, lest at any time thou dash thy foot against a stone. 12 And Jesus answering said unto him, It is said, Thou shalt not tempt the Lord thy God. 13 And when the devil had ended all the temptation, he departed from him for a season. LUKE 4:1-13 (KJV)

The Matthew passage is very similar in content to that of the Luke passage, but places temptations in a different order. With each temptation, the Lord gives a quotation from Scripture that addresses what our attitudes, motives, and desires should be.

With the first temptation of turning stones to bread, the Lord told Satan that we are to live for God and not for self. When Jesus was already hungry and the flesh was crying to be fed, this was not an easy choice to make. This was not an offensive move on the part of the Lord. He used Scripture to clarify His own thinking. It is worth noting that after the temptation Jesus was still hungry. Hunger is a response of the body to a need for food, much the same way that the body is aroused for other needs, such as sex. Resisting temptation does not remove the physical need, but it does put the fulfillment of that need in God's hands. Even as our Lord was tempted with a bodily function, but without sin, even so we may be tempted with an urge produced by a chemical reaction in our own bodies, but that does not mean that we have sinned. Temptation and sin are not the same thing.

With the second temptation of great worldly power if he would compromise his faith, Jesus forsook fame and fortune in favor of His relationship with God the Father. Knowing what His future held, this may not have been as tempting as it would be for some of us, but in worldly terms this is pretty big. Again, the Lord did not go on the offensive, but chose to use the Word of God to forsake temporal things that were in opposition to spiritual wellbeing. In the latter days when the Man of Sin comes, he will be tempted with the same thing and shall fail the temptation.

In the final temptation, the Lord was tempted to use his position frivolously for personal benefit by casting Himself off the temple wall to the ground. His response to the Devil was very clear. He was not going to violate His relationship with God the Father through some frivolous action, and He used the Word of God to declare it. Notice that the Devil even used Scripture itself to justify His temptation. We see many wolves in sheeps' clothing behind the pulpit today. Men and women who twist the Scripture for their own gain while at the same time stumbling many of the saints of God.

PRAYER

What follows the Armor of God in the book of Ephesians is something very important. It is something that we are admonished to do for one another.

> *18 Praying always with all prayer and supplication in the Spirit, and watching thereunto with all perseverance and supplication for all saints; EPHESIANS 6:18 (KJV)*

This is our part in spiritual warfare: to pray for one another. It is not independent of God, but rather totally dependent on God. We cannot deal with a Devil that we cannot see. We must rely on God to do that. We can pray for those whom we know and for the trials that they go through, even as our Lord did for Simon Peter.

> 31 And the Lord said, Simon, Simon, behold, Satan hath desired to have
> you, that he may sift you as wheat: 32 But I have prayed for thee, that
> thy faith fail not: and when thou art converted, strengthen thy brethren.
> LUKE 22:31-32 (KJV)

We are admonished to follow the Lord's example in this by praying for one another.

The use of the Armor of God depends upon our ability to trust God by faith to deliver us from temptation. The Devil will not tap us on the shoulder to tell us what he is up to. Often, he catches us by surprise and we do not even realize that it is this subtle serpent that is tempting us. It is incumbent upon the saints to be aware of the temptations that afflict us.

> 8 Be sober, be vigilant; because your adversary the devil, as a roaring
> lion, walketh about, seeking whom he may devour: 9 Whom resist
> stedfast in the faith, knowing that the same afflictions are accomplished
> in your brethren that are in the world. 1 PETER 5:8-9 (KJV)

While the Devil is an external enemy that apparently has access to our thoughts, the other external enemy, the Satanic World System, has access to our senses. This will be described in the chapter to follow.

CHAPTER FOUR

OUR SPIRITUAL ENEMY–THE WORLD

CHAPTER 2 ADDRESSED our Spiritual Enemy the Flesh, and Chapter 3 addressed Our Spiritual Enemy the Devil. In Chapter 4, we will address what the Bible has to say about the Satanic World System as a Spiritual Enemy. The reader may be surprised at the all-encompassing nature of this spiritual enemy is.

THE WORLD IN THE BIBLE

There are two words in the New Testament translated as "world." One is the Greek word *kosmos,* which means an ordered system.[1] The other is a time-related word, *aion,* which can either mean eternity or a universal period of time usually referred to as an "age."[2] In this chapter, we will examine the world as an ordered system. In Chapter 5, we will look at the world as pertaining to "This Present Evil Age."

THE RELATIONSHIP OF THE DEVIL AND THE WORLD

Not every reference to *kosmos* is a reference to the Satanic World System, but there is a great deal of Scripture that relates the unsaved as being controlled by the Devil. Recalling from Chapter 3 and the history of the Devil, Satan is the controlling influence in the world today.

*18 We know that whosoever is born of God sinneth not; but he that is begotten of God keepeth himself, and that wicked one toucheth him not. 19 And we know that we are of God, and the whole world **(kosmos)** lieth in wickedness **(the wicked one)**. 1 JOHN 5:18-19 (KJV)*

The Lord Jesus clearly stated the relationship between the Devil and the world in the parable of the wheat and the tares.

*38 The field is the world **(kosmos)**; the good seed are the children of the kingdom; but the tares are the children of the wicked one; 39 The enemy that sowed them is the devil; the harvest is the end of the world **(aion)**; and the reapers are the angels. MATTHEW 13:38-39 (KJV)*

The Apostle Paul amplified our understanding of this relationship:

*1 And you hath he quickened, who were dead in trespasses and sins; 2 Wherein in time past ye walked according to the course of this world **(kosmos)**, according to the prince of the power of the air, the spirit that now worketh in the children of disobedience: 3 Among whom also we all had our conversation in times past in the lusts of our flesh, fulfilling the desires of the flesh and of the mind; and were by nature the children of wrath, even as others. EPHESIANS 2:1-3 (KJV)*

This is an important passage in understanding the power that the Devil exercises over the world. The title given for the Devil is "prince of the power of the air," thus demonstrating his ability to mimic the Holy

Spirit *(pneuma)* in the unsaved. The term "worketh" is *energeo*,[3] and it is used of the operation of the Lord in the believer's life as well.[4]

> *13 For it is God which worketh (energeo) in you both to will and to do of his good pleasure. PHILIPPIANS 2:13 (KJV)*

And

> *6 And there are diversities of operations, but it is the same God which worketh (energeo) all in all. 1 CORINTHIANS 12:6 (KJV)*

And

> *11 But all these worketh (energeo) that one and the selfsame Spirit, dividing to every man severally as he will. 1 CORINTHIANS 12:11 (KJV)*

And

> *18 The eyes of your understanding being enlightened; that ye may know what is the hope of his calling, and what the riches of the glory of his inheritance in the saints, 19 And what is the exceeding greatness of his power to usward who believe, according to the working (energeia[5]) of his mighty power, EPHESIANS 1:18-19 (KJV)*

And

> *8 For he that wrought effectually in Peter to the apostleship of the circumcision, the same was mighty (energeo) in me toward the Gentiles: GALATIANS 2:8 (KJV)*

And

*20 Now unto him that is able to do exceeding abundantly above all that we ask or think, according to the power that worketh **(energeo)** in us, EPHESIANS 3:20 (KJV)*

And

*29 Whereunto I also labour, striving according to his working, which worketh **(energeo)** in me mightily. COLOSSIANS 1:29 (KJV)*

All of these verses demonstrate the energizing power of God in the believer's life. In fact, we are promised that God is mightier than Satan.

3 And every spirit that confesseth not that Jesus Christ is come in the flesh is not of God: and this is that spirit of antichrist, whereof ye have heard that it should come; and even now already is it in the world. 4 Ye are of God, little children, and have overcome them: because greater is he that is in you, than he that is in the world. 1 JOHN 4:3-4 (KJV)

From Ephesians 2:1-3 it is apparent that the Devil controls (or energizes) the unsaved world much like the Holy Spirit controls the believer. The result is that the unsaved are "children of disobedience" and "children of wrath" who are "walking after the course of this world" and who have their conduct in the lust of their flesh and of the mind. This would indicate that Satan uses the enemy within every man, the Flesh or sin nature within, for controlling his activities. The result is a vast manipulated army we refer to as the Satanic World System.

SATAN'S METHODS FOR CONTROLLING THE WORLD

What methods does Satan use to control a vast number of people who do not even believe that he exists? Our Lord gave us an indication.

42 Jesus said unto them, If God were your Father, ye would love me: for I proceeded forth and came from God; neither came I of myself, but he sent me. 43 Why do ye not understand my speech? even because ye cannot hear my word. 44 Ye are of your father the devil, and the lusts of your father ye will do. He was a murderer from the beginning, and abode not in the truth, because there is no truth in him. When he speaketh a lie, he speaketh of his own: for he is a liar, and the father of it. 45 And because I tell you the truth, ye believe me not. JOHN 8:42-45 (KJV)

The Devil's greatest tool has always been the lie. The world swallows the lie because it hates the truth and loves evil.

19 And this is the condemnation, that light is come into the world, and men loved darkness rather than light, because their deeds were evil. 20 For every one that doeth evil hateth the light, neither cometh to the light, lest his deeds should be reproved. 21 But he that doeth truth cometh to the light, that his deeds may be made manifest, that they are wrought in God. JOHN 3:19-21 (KJV)

The Devil has another device in his arsenal to control the unsaved: blindness.

3 But if our gospel be hid, it is hid to them that are lost: 4 In whom the god of this world hath blinded the minds of them which believe not, lest the light of the glorious gospel of Christ, who is the image of God, should shine unto them. 2 CORINTHIANS 4:3-4 (KJV)

Note the Devil's title of "god of this world" who is able to blind the unsaved to the Gospel. This accomplishes his goal of luring man into independence from God.

17 This I say therefore, and testify in the Lord, that ye henceforth walk not as other Gentiles walk, in the vanity of their mind, 18 Having the understanding darkened, being alienated from the life of God through the ignorance that is in them, because of the blindness of their heart: 19 Who being past feeling have given themselves over unto lasciviousness, to work all uncleanness with greediness. EPHESIANS 4:17-19 (KJV)

The result of this independence is total sensuality. Sensuality leads to sin, and sin leads to the wrath of God.

18 For the wrath of God is revealed from heaven against all ungodliness and unrighteousness of men, who hold the truth in unrighteousness; 19 Because that which may be known of God is manifest in them; for God hath shewed it unto them. 20 For the invisible things of him from the creation of the world are clearly seen, being understood by the things that are made, even his eternal power and Godhead; so that they are without excuse: 21 Because that, when they knew God, they glorified him not as God, neither were thankful; but became vain in their imaginations, and their foolish heart was darkened. 22 Professing themselves to be wise, they became fools, 23 And changed the glory of the uncorruptible God into an image made like to corruptible man, and to birds, and fourfooted beasts, and creeping things. 24 Wherefore God also gave them up to uncleanness through the lusts of their own hearts, to dishonour their own bodies between themselves: 25 Who changed the truth of God into a lie, and worshipped and served the creature more than the Creator, who is blessed for ever. Amen. 26 For this cause God gave them up unto vile affections: for even their women did change the natural use into that which is against nature: 27 And likewise also the men, leaving the natural use of the woman, burned in their lust one toward another; men with men working that which is unseemly, and receiving in themselves that recompence of their error which was meet. 28 And even as they did not like to retain God in their knowledge, God gave them over to a reprobate mind, to do those things which are not convenient; 29 Being filled with all unrighteousness, fornication, wickedness, covetousness, maliciousness; full of envy, murder, debate, deceit, malignity; whisperers, 30 Backbiters, haters of God, despiteful, proud, boasters, inventors of evil things, disobedient to parents, 31 Without understanding, covenantbreakers, without natural affection, implacable, unmerciful: 32 Who knowing the judgment of God, that they which commit such things are worthy of death, not only do the same, but have pleasure in them that do them. ROMANS 1:18-32 (KJV)

Sensuality is the temptation of the world toward the believer. Worldly temptations come through the senses. It is not improper for the believer to use the things of the world. The things of the world are not sacred in themselves, and they wear out with use.

31 And they that use this world, as not abusing it: for the fashion of this world passeth away. 1 CORINTHIANS 7:31 (KJV)

The problem is not the use of the world; it is being used by the world for Satan's purposes.

THE WORLD AS A SPIRITUAL ENEMY

As a Spiritual Enemy, the world has nothing in common with the Christian.

3 Behold, what manner of love the Father hath bestowed upon us, that we should be called the sons of God: therefore the world knoweth us not, because it knew him not. 1 JOHN 3:1 (KJV)

It should not surprise us that the world hates believers.

13 Marvel not, my brethren, if the world hate you. 1 JOHN 3:13 (KJV)

The world hates the believer because of Christ, but loves its own.

18 If the world hate you, ye know that it hated me before it hated you. 19 If ye were of the world, the world would love his own: but because ye are not of the world, but I have chosen you out of the world, therefore the world hateth you. JOHN 15:18-19 (KJV)

It is not our place to hate the world, even though the world hates us.

16 For God so loved the world, that he gave his only begotten Son, that whosoever believeth in him should not perish, but have everlasting life. 17 For God sent not his Son into the world to condemn the world; but that the world through him might be saved. JOHN 3:16-17 (KJV)

Christ died for the sins of both the saved and the unsaved, thus making salvation possible for all.

2 And he is the propitiation for our sins: and not for ours only, but also for the sins of the whole world. 1 JOHN 2:2 (KJV)

It is evident then that the war is one sided as pertaining to animosity. Unfortunately, the world has its own attractions that stumble the believer.

WORLDLY TEMPTATION

The world uses its own wisdom and persuasion to lure the Christian away from God.

8 Beware lest any man spoil you through philosophy and vain deceit, after the tradition of men, after the rudiments of the world, and not after Christ. COLOSSIANS 2:8 (KJV)

The word "spoil" is as in "spoils of war." The verse is talking about taking away our riches in Christ. Many things of the world sound very logical and appealing. This is more a function of this evil age, and it will be dealt with in Chapter 5.

Worldly temptation comes through the senses. The world flaunts Works of the Flesh before believers to taunt us into losing fellowship with God. Addictions and improper sexuality are obvious sensual entice-ments. Others are corruptions of institutions within the world, such as business and government. Greed is also a worldly attraction.

10 For the love of money is the root of all evil: which while some coveted after, they have erred from the faith, and pierced themselves through with many sorrows. 1 TIMOTHY 6:10 (KJV)

The term "all" is present in the original Greek, but the leading article "the" is not. This would indicate that the love of money is a root of every category of evil, but it is not the only cause. Even in part it still equates to covetousness. The main means of enticement by the world is lust and pride. This is best seen in our defense against the world.

THE DEFENSE AGAINST THE WORLD

The problem with the world is that it steals or misdirects the love that God has given to the believer.

> *15 Love not the world, neither the things that are in the world. If any*
> *man love the world, the love of the Father is not in him. 16 For all that*
> *is in the world, the lust of the flesh, and the lust of the eyes, and the*
> *pride of life, is not of the Father, but is of the world. 17 And the world*
> *passeth away, and the lust thereof: but he that doeth the will of God*
> *abideth for ever. 1 JOHN 2:15-17 (KJV)*

Love is the first of the attitudes that God gives the believer as a defense against sin:

> *22 But the fruit of the Spirit is love, joy, peace, longsuffering, gentleness,*
> *goodness, faith, 23 Meekness, temperance: against such there is no law.*
> *GALATIANS 5:22-23 (KJV)*

The world entices the believer to misdirect the love that God has provided to them and place it in the things of the world, such as lust and pride. This is not always in the form of something that appears to be evil in itself. It can be very humanitarian, such as a social gospel. It can also be disguised as duty, such as the atheistic education of children in the public school system. Being alert enough to properly direct God-given love is the defense against the world.

> *27 Pure religion and undefiled before God and the Father is this, To*
> *visit the fatherless and widows in their affliction, and to keep himself*
> *unspotted from the world. JAMES 1:27 (KJV)*

The believer is to do good things, but only as directed by God being led of the Holy Spirit to do so. The defense of love is therefore a supernatural defense. Once again, the believer must depend upon God for deliverance. Our own efforts apart from the working of the Holy Spirit are futile at best. God provides a godly outcome to worldly problems. Man provides a self-centered outcome to worldly problems. Therefore walking by means of the Holy Spirit is essential for victory over the world.

VICTORY OVER THE WORLD

Our victory over the world rests in who we are in relationship to God. It does not rest in eloquence or craftiness. It rests in love, truth, and obedience to the call of God to believe on the Lord Jesus Christ.

> 2 By this we know that we love the children of God, when we love God, and keep his commandments. 3 For this is the love of God, that we keep his commandments: and his commandments are not grievous. 4 For whatsoever is born of God overcometh the world: and this is the victory that overcometh the world, even our faith. 5 Who is he that overcometh the world, but he that believeth that Jesus is the Son of God? 6 This is he that came by water and blood, even Jesus Christ; not by water only, but by water and blood. And it is the Spirit that beareth witness, because the Spirit is truth. 1 JOHN 5:2-6 (KJV)

The grace God gives by our faith has saved us and that same grace by faith can keep us in times of worldly temptations. The Satanic World System can only be overcome by the power of the Cross and the love of God. In looking at the "Works of the Flesh" as described in Chapter 6, some are improper attitudes, some are actions, and some are what are considered today to be "addiction." The term addiction usually receives the status of an illness or disease. If instead it is viewed as activities of the sin nature brought about by a worldly temptation through the senses, then we have every hope of overcoming the sin. Behaviors such as drunkenness, drug use, homosexuality, compulsive theft, or whatever the sin, all of these can be controlled by the power of the Holy Spirit—without exception. But if we love the sin instead of loving God, we will be consumed by the activities of sin.

18 And be not drunk with wine, wherein is excess; but be filled with the Spirit; EPHESIANS 5:18-19 (KJV)

We are either controlled by certain sins or we are controlled by the Holy Spirit. Wherein does our love lie? In this University of Life, we do not all major on the same sins, but we all have our favorite sins.

8 If we say that we have no sin, we deceive ourselves, and the truth is not in us. 1 JOHN 1:8 (KJV)

Neither can we say that sin has not affected us because we all live with the World all around us.

10 If we say that we have not sinned, we make him a liar, and his word is not in us. 1 JOHN 1:10 (KJV)

It is only by declaring our inadequacy before God to overcome sin that we can achieve victory over sin by the Blood of Jesus Christ.

9 If we confess our sins, he is faithful and just to forgive us our sins, and to cleanse us from all unrighteousness. 1 JOHN 1:9 (KJV)

None of us is strong enough to overcome any of our Spiritual Enemies on our own. It must be done by the power of God.

PART TWO

THE BATTLEGROUND

He Hideth My Soul

Words: Fanny J. Crosby
Music: William J. Kirkpatrick
Based on Exodus 33:22

A wonderful Savior is Jesus my Lord,
A wonderful Savior to me;
He hideth my soul in the cleft of the rock,
Where rivers of pleasure I see.

Refrain:

He hideth my soul in the cleft of the rock,
That shadows a dry, thirsty land;
He hideth my life in the depths of His love,
And covers me there with His hand,
And covers me there with His hand.

A wonderful Savior is Jesus my Lord,
He taketh my burden away,
He holdeth me up and I shall not be moved,
He giveth me strength as my day.

With numberless blessings each moment He crowns,
And filled with His fullness divine,
I sing in my rapture, oh, glory to God!
For such a Redeemer as mine.

When clothed with His brightness transported I rise
To meet Him in clouds of the sky,
His perfect salvation, His wonderful love,
I'll shout with the millions on high.

CHAPTER FIVE

THIS PRESENT EVIL AGE

THE LORD IS OUR REFUGE and He is able to keep our souls in this present world. This could apply to either the Satanic World System or to This Present Evil Age. One of the things that helps us through the trials of this Earth is the hope of better things to come.

> *14 Let not your heart be troubled: ye believe in God, believe also in me. 2 In my Father's house are many mansions: if it were not so, I would have told you. I go to prepare a place for you. 3 And if I go and prepare a place for you, I will come again, and receive you unto myself; that where I am, there ye may be also. 4 And whither I go ye know, and the way ye know. JOHN 14:1-4 KJV*

In Part 1 of the book, we looked at our Spiritual Enemies: the World, the Flesh, and the Devil, albeit not in that order. In Part 2, we will look at the location of the battle and our interaction with it. The location of the battle is in the mind, but it has many external influences. This part looks at the world as seen from the Bible in this period of time called an "age" and its external influences on the believer. There are many ages defined in the Bible, but for our purposes we will focus on just two: the Age of Grace and This Present Evil Age.

THE AGES AND THE BIBLE

As stated in Chapter 4, there are two words in the New Testament translated as "world." One is the Greek word **kosmos,** which means an ordered system.[1] Chapter 4 dealt with the world as an ordered system controlled by Satan. It was found that the believer is enticed to direct the love that God has given him away from the things of the Lord (1 John 2:15-17) and toward the base elements of the world. When this happens, the believer loses the ability to produce the love of God as a fruit of the Spirit (Galatians 5:22-23), and he falls out of fellowship with God because he is no longer walking by the Spirit of God (Galatians 5:16-17). At that point, any manner of Works of the Flesh can result. As with anything that draws us away from God, confession and restoration are required (1 John 1:9).

The other use of the term "world" is a time-related word, **aion,** which can either mean eternity or a universal period of time usually referred to as an "age".[2] There are many ages in the Bible. Some of these are consecutive in time, and some run parallel in time. Examples of consecutive ages are:

- The Age of Law – This was the period from the giving of the Law on Mt. Sinai to the Crucifixion of Jesus (Luke 1:70, Acts 3:21).

- The Age of Grace – We are in this period today. It was hidden in Christ from the beginning of time (Ephesians 3:1-20). This age will continue until the Lord's return for His Church (1 Corinthians 11:26).

- The Kingdom Age – This is a time yet to come when Christ shall reign upon the Earth, sitting on the throne of David (Isaiah 9:6-7).

The ages above were put in place by God to demonstrate His holy attributes before man. There is an age that runs parallel to the demonstration of God's grace, mercy, justice, and faithfulness. This is an age in which man operates according to his own sinful, wicked, rotten flesh. It is called This Present Evil Age, and it contrasts the goodness of God with the sinfulness of man.

*3 Grace be to you and peace from God the Father, and from our Lord Jesus Christ, 4 Who gave himself for our sins, that he might deliver us from this present evil world **(aion)**, according to the will of God and our Father: GALATIANS 1:3-4 (KJV)*

THIS PRESENT EVIL AGE

This Present Evil Age has many characteristics that are unique. This age started in the Garden of Eden with the fall of man.

*12 Wherefore, as by one man sin entered into the world **(kosmos)**, and death by sin; and so death passed upon all men, for that all have sinned: ROMANS 5:12 (KJV)*

This Present Evil Age has a god of its own whom they worship not. It is the Devil.

*3 But if our gospel be hid, it is hid to them that are lost: 4 In whom the god of this world **(aion)** hath blinded the minds of them which believe not, lest the light of the glorious gospel of Christ, who is the image of God, should shine unto them. 2 CORINTHIANS 4:3-4 (KJV)*

As previously stated, the Devil rules this age.

11 Put on the whole armour of God, that ye may be able to stand against the wiles of the devil. 12 For we wrestle not against flesh and blood, but against principalities, against powers, against the rulers of the darkness of this world (aion), against spiritual wickedness in high places. Ephesians 6:11-12 (KJV)

This age has its own wisdom and the Christian is not to hold onto it.

18 Let no man deceive himself. If any man among you seemeth to be wise in this world (aion), let him become a fool, that he may be wise. 19 For the wisdom of this world (aion) is foolishness with God. For it is written, He taketh the wise in their own craftiness. 20 And again, The Lord knoweth the thoughts of the wise, that they are vain. 21 Therefore let no man glory in men. For all things are yours; 22 Whether Paul, or Apollos, or Cephas, or the world (kosmos), or life, or death, or things present, or things to come; all are yours; 23 And ye are Christ's; and Christ is God's. 1 CORINTHIANS 3:18-23 (KJV)

The Christian's hope must never rest in man. It must rest in Christ alone. Even so, the people of this age are very intelligent, as our Lord has warned us in the Parable of the Unjust Steward.

8 And the lord commended the unjust steward, because he had done wisely: for the children of this world (aion) are in their generation wiser than the children of light. LUKE 16:8 (KJV)

It should be evident that the believer has little in common with the people of This Present Evil Age, yet it is the philosophies of this age that stumble the Christian the most.

THE PHILOSOPHY OF THIS AGE

There is a term used to distinguish between that which is sacred or religious and that which is supposedly neutral to religion. The term is "secular." Secular comes from the Latin word **saeculum,** and it means "an age."[3] **Saeculum** is the Latin equivalent of the Greek word **aion.** In every quarter of American society, those things that are "secular" are thought to be neutral to spiritual things. But the Bible warns the believer:

> 2 And be not conformed to this world **(aion)**: but be ye transformed by the renewing of your mind, that ye may prove what is that good, and acceptable, and perfect, will of God. ROMANS 12:2 (KJV)

If we are not to be "conformed to this age," then we are not to be secular in our understanding. This can only be accomplished through the renewing of our minds by the finished work of Jesus Christ on Calvary's Cross. As our "old man" is reckoned "nailed to the cross" (Romans 6:6), our sin nature is subdued by the power of the Holy Spirit (Galatians 5:16). One of the major lies of the Devil concerning this age is that children are to be taught in a government school system that is "secular" and devoid of "religion." Devoid of content relating to God makes the education "atheistic" and not neutral. Atheism is the religion of this age because it is in opposition to God. Therefore, taking pride in "secularism" is to live in opposition to God. There are other statements concerning the philosophy of this age.

> 8 Beware lest any man spoil you through philosophy and vain deceit, after the tradition of men, after the rudiments of the world **(aion)**, and not after Christ. COLOSSIANS 2:8 (KJV)

The term "spoil" is as in "spoils of war." The admonition is to be aware that the Satanic World System will trick the Christian into giving up their treasure in Christ by secular means. The children of this age will go out of their way to deny God credit for His handy work.

3 Knowing this first, that there shall come in the last days scoffers, walking after their own lusts, 4 And saying, Where is the promise of his coming? for since the fathers fell asleep, all things continue as they were from the beginning of the creation. 5 For this they willingly are ignorant of, that by the word of God the heavens were of old, and the earth standing out of the water and in the water: 6 Whereby the world that then was, being overflowed with water, perished: 7 But the heavens and the earth, which are now, by the same word are kept in store, reserved unto fire against the day of judgment and perdition of ungodly men. 2 PETER 3:3-7 (KJV)

To avoid crediting God for His creation, the children of this age are "willfully ignorant" and "scoff" at God. They have replaced the glory of God with random chance and evolution. These secular speculations are touted as science, even in the absence of proof as well as contradictions in probability. This same concept of physical evolution has crept into legal systems, governance, education, and all manner of decision making. Unfortunately, an analysis of "social evolution" is beyond this writing, but it is a definite tool of the Satanic World System in its efforts to stumble the child of God. It manifests itself as situational ethics, conflict resolution, values clarification, behavior modification, and even apologetics.

CHAPTER SIX

RULES OF ENGAGEMENT

AS QUANTITATIVE PERIODS OF TIME, ages are not considered as Spiritual Enemies. They are not causes in themselves, but rather periods of time when certain conditions are found to exist. There are no defenses required for an age because time itself is a physical variable that exists in the context of God's creation. There are, however, rules of engagement for conditions found in This Present Evil Age.

WALK BY THE SPIRIT

The first rule of engagement is to walk by the Spirit of God and remain in His control. Every physical test should be viewed as a spiritual opportunity.

> *1 Therefore being justified by faith, we have peace with God through our Lord Jesus Christ: 2 By whom also we have access by faith into this grace wherein we stand, and rejoice in hope of the glory of God. 3 And not only so, but we glory in tribulations also: knowing that tribulation worketh patience; 4 And patience, experience; and experience, hope: 5 And hope maketh not ashamed; because the love of God is shed abroad in our hearts by the Holy Ghost which is given unto us. ROMANS 5:1-5 (KJV)*

This world is our boot camp to get us fitted for Heaven. Contrary to our thinking, it does not require self-reliance. It requires faith in God and His abilities. We should welcome the opportunity to trust God. Tribulation is the testing of trust and it yields character.

AVOID EVIL

The admonishment to avoid evil is not unique to the New Testament. Solomon admonished his son not to keep company with evildoers.

10 My son, if sinners entice thee, consent thou not. 11 If they say, Come with us, let us lay wait for blood, let us lurk privily for the innocent without cause: 12 Let us swallow them up alive as the grave; and whole, as those that go down into the pit: 13 We shall find all precious substance, we shall fill our houses with spoil: 14 Cast in thy lot among us; let us all have one purse: 15 My son, walk not thou in the way with them; refrain thy foot from their path: 16 For their feet run to evil, and make haste to shed blood. 17 Surely in vain the net is spread in the sight of any bird. 18 And they lay wait for their own blood; they lurk privily for their own lives. 19 So are the ways of every one that is greedy of gain; which taketh away the life of the owners thereof. PROVERBS 1:10-20 (KJV)

The New Testament bridges this same concept with Old Testament examples.

1 Moreover, brethren, I would not that ye should be ignorant, how that all our fathers were under the cloud, and all passed through the sea; 2 And were all baptized unto Moses in the cloud and in the sea; 3 And did all eat the same spiritual meat; 4 And did all drink the same spiritual drink: for they drank of that spiritual Rock that followed them: and that

Rock was Christ. 5 But with many of them God was not well pleased: for they were overthrown in the wilderness. 6 Now these things were our examples, to the intent we should not lust after evil things, as they also lusted. 7 Neither be ye idolaters, as were some of them; as it is written, The people sat down to eat and drink, and rose up to play. 8 Neither let us commit fornication, as some of them committed, and fell in one day three and twenty thousand. 9 Neither let us tempt Christ, as some of them also tempted, and were destroyed of serpents. 10 Neither murmur ye, as some of them also murmured, and were destroyed of the destroyer. 11 Now all these things happened unto them for ensamples: and they are written for our admonition, upon whom the ends of the world are come. 12 Wherefore let him that thinketh he standeth take heed lest he fall. 13 There hath no temptation taken you but such as is common to man: but God is faithful, who will not suffer you to be tempted above that ye are able; but will with the temptation also make a way to escape, that ye may be able to bear it. 14 Wherefore, my dearly beloved, flee from idolatry. 1 CORINTHIANS 10:1-14 (KJV)

It would be extremely easy to view these things as a reinstatement of the law. They are actually an admonition to recognize sin and see it as God sees it. The passage also encourages us to recognize the spiritual tools and blessings that God gives us as He had given them to the nation of Israel. The passage also includes the promise of restraint in temptation so that we will not be required to endure testing that is past our abilities to overcome in the Lord. We are also admonished to recognized our relationship to God as a means of avoiding sin.

12 All things are lawful unto me, but all things are not expedient: all things are lawful for me, but I will not be brought under the power of any. 13 Meats for the belly, and the belly for meats: but God shall destroy both it and them. Now the body is not for fornication, but for the Lord; and the Lord for the body. 14 And God hath both raised up the Lord, and will also raise up us by his own power. 15 Know ye not that your bodies are the members of Christ? shall I then take the members of Christ, and make them the members of an harlot? God forbid. 16 What? know ye not that he which is joined to an harlot is one body? for two, saith he, shall be one flesh. 17 But he that is joined unto the Lord is one spirit. 18 Flee fornication. Every sin that a man doeth is without the body; but he that committeth fornication sinneth against his own body. 19 What? know ye not that your body is the temple of the Holy Ghost which is in you, which ye have of God, and ye are not your own? 20 For ye are bought with a price: therefore glorify God in your body, and in your spirit, which are God's. 1 CORINTHIANS 6:12-20 (KJV)

Because the Holy Spirit now inhabits the mortal bodies of Christians, we are to provide Him with a suitable habitation, holy and free of sin. We see the same concept in other passages, including the following:

14 Be ye not unequally yoked together with unbelievers: for what fellowship hath righteousness with unrighteousness? and what communion hath light with darkness? 15 And what concord hath Christ with Belial? or what part hath he that believeth with an infidel? 16 And what agreement hath the temple of God with idols? for ye are the temple of the living God; as God hath said, I will dwell in them, and walk in them; and I will be their God, and they shall be my people. 17 Wherefore come out from among them, and be ye separate, saith the Lord, and touch not the unclean thing; and I will receive you, 18 And will be a Father unto you, and ye shall be my sons and daughters, saith the Lord Almighty. 2 CORINTHIANS 6:14-18 (KJV)

The believer is therefore responsible for maintaining his fellowship with God and to avoid unhealthy associations with the world. But what are believers to do when the world is in their faces with sin?

REPROVE SIN

There are times when sin is presented before the Christian in whatever form and the Christian must respond to it.

> *Be ye therefore followers of God, as dear children; 2 And walk in love, as Christ also hath loved us, and hath given himself for us an offering and a sacrifice to God for a sweetsmelling savour. 3 But fornication, and all uncleanness, or covetousness, let it not be once named among you, as becometh saints; 4 Neither filthiness, nor foolish talking, nor jesting, which are not convenient: but rather giving of thanks. 5 For this ye know, that no whoremonger, nor unclean person, nor covetous man, who is an idolater, hath any inheritance in the kingdom of Christ and of God. 6 Let no man deceive you with vain words: for because of these things cometh the wrath of God upon the children of disobedience. 7 Be not ye therefore partakers with them. 8 For ye were sometimes darkness, but now are ye light in the Lord: walk as children of light: 9 (For the fruit of the Spirit is in all goodness and righteousness and truth;) 10 Proving what is acceptable unto the Lord. 11 And have no fellowship with the unfruitful works of darkness, but rather reprove them. 12 For it is a shame even to speak of those things which are done of them in secret. 13 But all things that are reproved are made manifest by the light: for whatsoever doth make manifest is light. EPHESIANS 5:1-13 (KJV)*

This passage can be separated out into six basic steps:

1. Choose according to godly principles. Verses 1 - 2.

2. Recognize sin. Verses 3 - 6.

3. Do not partake of sin. Verse 7.

4. Be led of the Spirit and do right. Verses 8 - 10.

5. Do not compromise, barter, or reconcile away that which is right. Verse 11a.

6. Be used as a tool of God to expose evil. Versed 11b - 13

There are times when a Christian can no longer be passive. It is important to represent sin as what it is and to say so out loud. The world is as lost as we once were, and not declaring sin to be sinful does them no favors before a righteous and holy God. Christians should implore all to recognize their sin and accept the mercy and cleansing from evil that only the Blood of Jesus Christ can endlessly supply.

THE CHURCH IS TO POLICE ITS OWN

The Body of Christ is to settle matters within itself, but we are not required to right every wrong for the world. Nor are we required to stop living in this world.

9 I wrote unto you in an epistle not to company with fornicators: 10 Yet not altogether with the fornicators of this world, or with the covetous, or extortioners, or with idolaters; for then must ye needs go out of the world. 11 But now I have written unto you not to keep company, if any man that is called a brother be a fornicator, or covetous, or an idolater, or a railer, or a drunkard, or an extortioner; with such an one no not to eat. 12 For what have I to do to judge them also that are without? do not ye judge them that are within? 13 But them that are without God judgeth. Therefore put away from among yourselves that wicked person. 1 CORINTHIANS 5:9-13 (KJV)

The Church is required to deal with grievous sin in its midst, but what does that entail?

It is reported commonly that there is fornication among you, and such fornication as is not so much as named among the Gentiles, that one should have his father's wife. 2 And ye are puffed up, and have not rather mourned, that he that hath done this deed might be taken away from among you. 3 For I verily, as absent in body, but present in spirit, have judged already, as though I were present, concerning him that hath so done this deed, 4 In the name of our Lord Jesus Christ, when ye are gathered together, and my spirit, with the power of our Lord Jesus Christ, 5 To deliver such an one unto Satan for the destruction of the flesh, that the spirit may be saved in the day of the Lord Jesus. 6 Your glorying is not good. Know ye not that a little leaven leaveneth the whole lump? 7 Purge out therefore the old leaven, that ye may be a new lump, as ye are unleavened. For even Christ our passover is sacrificed for us: 8 Therefore let us keep the feast, not with old leaven, neither with the leaven of malice and wickedness; but with the unleavened bread of sincerity and truth. 1 CORINTHIANS 5:1-8 (KJV)

The Church is not a legal body, nor does it have prisons or anything that could be useful for punishment. The Church is a free and voluntary association. As such it is also free to disassociate as well. The admonition is to make it clear that the Church, as the temple of the Holy Spirit, will not participate in or lend credibility to the bad behavior of other believers. Obviously, we are all sinners. The fact that some believers major on sins that are more shocking than others does not diminish the sins of those casting judgment. The difference is in the goal. It should be the goal of the believer to maintain fellowship with God, and to help others to do the same. This reconciliation carries a warning:

> Brethren, if a man be overtaken in a fault, ye which are spiritual, restore such an one in the spirit of meekness; considering thyself, lest thou also be tempted. 2 Bear ye one another's burdens, and so fulfil the law of Christ. GALATIANS 6:1-2 (KJV)

Even though restoration is the goal, some Churches take great pride in their separation. There are jokes about some Churches being so separated that they don't even talk to themselves. There is a point where repentance must be recognized.

> 5 But if any have caused grief, he hath not grieved me, but in part: that I may not overcharge you all. 6 Sufficient to such a man is this punishment, which was inflicted of many. 7 So that contrariwise ye ought rather to forgive him, and comfort him, lest perhaps such a one should be swallowed up with overmuch sorrow. 8 Wherefore I beseech you that ye would confirm your love toward him. 9 For to this end also did I write, that I might know the proof of you, whether ye be obedient in all things. 10 To whom ye forgive any thing, I forgive also: for if I forgave any thing, to whom I forgave it, for your sakes forgave I it in the person of Christ; 11 Lest Satan should get an advantage of us: for we are not ignorant of his devices. 2 CORINTHIANS 2:5-11 (KJV)

It does the Church no good to assume everyone in its body will be perfect all the time. Kicking other believers to the curb as garbage fit only for a landfill does nothing in itself to recover a troubled soul. Encouraging others to maintain fellowship with God and with each other does demonstrate the means of spirituality. Not that we can overcome sin on our own, but that through the finished work of Christ we can be more than conquerors over sin.

> 37 Nay, in all these things we are more than conquerors through him that loved us. 38 For I am persuaded, that neither death, nor life, nor angels, nor principalities, nor powers, nor things present, nor things to come, 39 Nor height, nor depth, nor any other creature, shall be able to separate us from the love of God, which is in Christ Jesus our Lord. ROMANS 8:37-39 (KJV)

THE CHURCH MUST SETTLE ITS OWN DISPUTES

We live in a litigation-happy society where anyone can sue anybody over anything at any time. The Church is not immune to this, as it was not in the days of the Apostle Paul.

> 1 Dare any of you, having a matter against another, go to law before the unjust, and not before the saints? 2 Do ye not know that the saints shall judge the world? and if the world shall be judged by you, are ye unworthy to judge the smallest matters? 3 Know ye not that we shall judge angels? how much more things that pertain to this life? 4 If then ye have judgments of things pertaining to this life, set them to judge who are least esteemed in the church. 5 I speak to your shame. Is it so, that there is not a wise man among you? no, not one that shall be able to judge between his brethren? 6 But brother goeth to law with brother, and that before the unbelievers. 7 Now therefore there is utterly a fault among you, because ye go to law one with another. Why do ye not rather take wrong? why do ye not rather suffer yourselves to be defrauded? 8 Nay, ye do wrong, and defraud, and that your brethren. 9 Know ye not that the unrighteous shall not inherit the kingdom of God? Be not

deceived: neither fornicators, nor idolaters, nor adulterers, nor effem-
inate, nor abusers of themselves with mankind, 10 Nor thieves, nor
covetous, nor drunkards, nor revilers, nor extortioners, shall inherit
the kingdom of God. 11 And such were some of you: but ye are washed,
but ye are sanctified, but ye are justified in the name of the Lord Jesus,
and by the Spirit of our God. 1 CORINTHIANS 6:1-11 (KJV)

Very few Churches have taken up the challenge of maintaining harmony within the body by helping members to work through their differences. This is most true in the area of marital affairs. The Church has all but abandoned the family, and marriage in particular, as an institution created by God in the Garden of Eden (Genesis 2:24-25). Marriage is viewed by most churches as an institution that is created and regulated by the government. With that the Church has tended to wash its hands of any interest in keeping families together. Addressing issues such as whose mule kicked who is minor in comparison to protecting the institutions of God. Until the Church takes an active interest in preserving the family, it is doubtful that any other disputes will be taken care of. The Church is quickly abandoning major portions of its role in the believer's life and giving them over to the government as part of the Satanic World System.

THE CHURCH PROVIDES STABLE TEACHING

There are good teachers and there are not as good teachers, but believers are not to abide the false teachers. The Spirit of God provides the Church with everything that it needs

11 And he gave some, apostles; and some, prophets; and some, evange-
lists; and some, pastors and teachers; 12 For the perfecting of the saints,
for the work of the ministry, for the edifying of the body of Christ: 13
Till we all come in the unity of the faith, and of the knowledge of the

100

*Son of God, unto a perfect man, unto the measure of the stature of the
fulness of Christ: 14 That we henceforth be no more children, tossed to
and fro, and carried about with every wind of doctrine, by the sleight
of men, and cunning craftiness, whereby they lie in wait to deceive;
15 But speaking the truth in love, may grow up into him in all things,
which is the head, even Christ: EPHESIANS 4:11-15 KJV*

The Church, being the pillar and ground of the truth (1 Timothy 3:15),
has been designed by God to teach everything that is necessary for life
and godliness. The teaching of the Word of God brings stability, and
the messengers of God are to bring that message. Where the Church
maintains what God has given, it will maintain stability. Not all teachers
are following the Scripture and doing their duty even though, if they are
believers, God has equipped them to do so. The four things that bring
the Church to its knees are as follows:

1. Teaching that gain is godliness, better known as the prosperity
    gospel

2. Teaching law over grace, better known as legalism

3. Acquiescing to sin as normal behavior, better known as
    lasciviousness

4. Despising or altering the Word of God for personal advantage,
    better known as heresy

All of these teachings in one way or another pervert the Word of God
to conform doctrine to This Present Evil Age. Those who subscribe to
such things should be shown the door and escorted out.

1 But there were false prophets also among the people, even as there shall be false teachers among you, who privily shall bring in damnable heresies, even denying the Lord that bought them, and bring upon themselves swift destruction. 2 And many shall follow their pernicious ways; by reason of whom the way of truth shall be evil spoken of. 3 And through covetousness shall they with feigned words make merchandise of you: whose judgment now of a long time lingereth not, and their damnation slumbereth not. 2 PETER 2:1-3 (KJV)

If you read on to the end of the chapter, this is one area where God encourages name calling. This not the only place:

10 But these speak evil of those things which they know not: but what they know naturally, as brute beasts, in those things they corrupt themselves. 11 Woe unto them! for they have gone in the way of Cain, and ran greedily after the error of Balaam for reward, and perished in the gainsaying of Core. 12 These are spots in your feasts of charity, when they feast with you, feeding themselves without fear: clouds they are without water, carried about of winds; trees whose fruit withereth, without fruit, twice dead, plucked up by the roots; 13 Raging waves of the sea, foaming out their own shame; wandering stars, to whom is reserved the blackness of darkness for ever. JUDE 10-13 (KJV)

If you are in a Church with someone like this in the pulpit, get out and do not look back.

REPENTANCE AND COMPASSION

We have seen that the Church is not to put up with intentional sin, but what about the repentant, the enslaved to sin (prostitutes), or the chemically trapped (drug users). There are those who want to come to

Christ and turn their lives around. The Bible indicates that this is the initial state of every believer:

> 9 *Know ye not that the unrighteous shall not inherit the kingdom of God? Be not deceived: neither fornicators, nor idolaters, nor adulterers, nor effeminate, nor abusers of themselves with mankind, 10 Nor thieves, nor covetous, nor drunkards, nor revilers, nor extortioners, shall inherit the kingdom of God. 11 And such were some of you: but ye are washed, but ye are sanctified, but ye are justified in the name of the Lord Jesus, and by the Spirit of our God. 1 CORINTHIANS 6:9-11 (KJV)*

A new believer is a new believer. They need to be trained in the faith as a babe in Christ. There are others who have been enslaved by men to do their bidding, and that bondage for sinful purposes is very real. Nowhere is this more profound than in the sex trafficking industry. Young girls in particular are sold into sex. Bringing them out of such a life to freedom in Christ can still come with heavy condemnation, as unjust as it may be. Wherever we find believers we should help them out of the bondages of sin, even as was done for Rahab the harlot in the Old Testament. Those who believe should be welcomed regardless of their humble estate.

> 31 *By faith the harlot Rahab perished not with them that believed not, when she had received the spies with peace. HEBREWS 11:31 (KJV)*

And

> 25 *Likewise also was not Rahab the harlot justified by works, when she had received the messengers, and had sent them out another way? JAMES 2:25 (KJV)*

And what of those trapped by the addictions of alcohol or drugs? These entrapments create physical dependencies. Much of the drug addictions we see are created by doctors who abuse prescription drugs (**pharmakeia**). We will learn more of this Work of the Flesh later, but the believer has direct access to the remedy.

> *16 This I say then, Walk in the Spirit, and ye shall not fulfil the lust of the flesh. GALATIANS 516 (KJV)*

The remedy for all Works of the Flesh is the same. The Spirit of God truly is the all-prevailing remedy. If a believer requires help getting out of sins' bondage, then the Church should unite behind them. Repentance demands forgiveness, reconciliation, and restoration.

CHAPTER SEVEN

THE SIN THAT SO EASILY BESETS US

SIN IS SOMETHING THAT PLAGUES us all because we all have the same sin nature. Both Leviticus and Deuteronomy in the Old Testament lay out in detail what behavior God expected of the Nation Israel. In the New Testament, many of these things are reiterated and some additions are made in the way of actions and attitudes to avoid. It is important to remember that Christ has already died to redeem us from our evil deeds. It is still up to us to accept what Christ has done, repent, and seek forgiveness, reconciliation, and restoration of fellowship with God. Starting from the listing of the Works of the Flesh in Galatians 5, what the Bible declares to be sin for the believer is examined.

> 19 Now the works of the flesh are manifest, which are these; Adultery, fornication, uncleanness, lasciviousness, 20 Idolatry, witchcraft, hatred, variance, emulations, wrath, strife, seditions, heresies, 21 Envyings, murders, drunkenness, revellings, and such like: of the which I tell you before, as I have also told you in time past, that they which do such things shall not inherit the kingdom of God. GALATIANS 5:19-21 (KJV)

ADULTERY (MOICHEIA)

The only way that the word ***moicheia*** is translated in the New Testament is "adultery."[1] It means to have sex with someone other than a spouse. The definition in the New Testament was broadened by our Lord Himself from that given in the Old Testament to include divorce.

> *2 And the Pharisees came to him, and asked him, Is it lawful for a man to put away his wife? tempting him. 3 And he answered and said unto them, What did Moses command you? 4 And they said, Moses suffered to write a bill of divorcement, and to put her away. 5 And Jesus answered and said unto them, For the hardness of your heart he wrote you this precept. 6 But from the beginning of the creation God made them male and female. 7 For this cause shall a man leave his father and mother, and cleave to his wife; 8 And they twain shall be one flesh: so then they are no more twain, but one flesh. 9 What therefore God hath joined together, let not man put asunder. 10 And in the house his disciples asked him again of the same matter. 11 And he saith unto them, Whosoever shall put away his wife, and marry another, committeth adultery against her. 12 And if a woman shall put away her husband, and be married to another, she committeth adultery. MARK 10:2-12 (KJV)*

This passage is very similar to Matthew 19:3-9. The same idea is advanced in Matthew 5:31-32 and in Luke 16:18. In modern times, it has become fashionable to view this as just a onetime event, but the Bible is clear that adultery can be an ongoing behavior.

> *2 For the woman which hath an husband is bound by the law to her husband so long as he liveth; but if the husband be dead, she is loosed*

from the law of her husband. 3 So then if, while her husband liveth, she be married to another man, she shall be called an adulteress: but if her husband be dead, she is free from that law; so that she is no adulteress, though she be married to another man. ROMANS 7:2-3 (KJV)

This is possibly the most overlooked sin in or out of the Church. Shallowness of commitment and an unwillingness to maintain responsibility are an ongoing problem.

FORNICATION (PORNEIA)

Porneia is normally translated as fornication, but its actual meanings include harlotry, adultery, fornication, homosexuality, lesbianism, intercourse with animals, incest, or anything associated with sexually deviant behavior.[2] In the Old Testament, such behavior always meant a condemnation and a sentence of death, usually by stoning. Some descriptions are given in the Old and New Testaments of God's attitudes towards such behavior. The New Testament describes God's attitude towards such behavior in detail.

18 For the wrath of God is revealed from heaven against all ungodliness and unrighteousness of men, who hold the truth in unrighteousness; 19 Because that which may be known of God is manifest in them; for God hath shewed it unto them. 20 For the invisible things of him from the creation of the world are clearly seen, being understood by the things that are made, even his eternal power and Godhead; so that they are without excuse: 21 Because that, when they knew God, they glorified him not as God, neither were thankful; but became vain in their imaginations, and their foolish heart was darkened. 22 Professing themselves to be wise, they became fools, 23 And changed the glory of the uncorruptible God into an image made like to corruptible man, and to birds, and fourfooted beasts, and creeping things.

24 Wherefore God also gave them up to uncleanness through the lusts of their own hearts, to dishonour their own bodies between themselves: 25 Who changed the truth of God into a lie, and worshipped and served the creature more than the Creator, who is blessed for ever. Amen.

26 For this cause God gave them up unto vile affections: for even their women did change the natural use into that which is against nature: 27 And likewise also the men, leaving the natural use of the woman, burned in their lust one toward another; men with men working that which is unseemly, and receiving in themselves that recompence of their error which was meet.

28 And even as they did not like to retain God in their knowledge, God gave them over to a reprobate mind, to do those things which are not convenient; 29 Being filled with all unrighteousness, fornication, wickedness, covetousness, maliciousness; full of envy, murder, debate, deceit, malignity; whisperers, 30 Backbiters, haters of God, despiteful, proud, boasters, inventors of evil things, disobedient to parents, 31 Without understanding, covenantbreakers, without natural affection, implacable, unmerciful: 32 Who knowing the judgment of God, that they which commit such things are worthy of death, not only do the same, but have pleasure in them that do them. ROMANS 1:18-32 (KJV)

Those who believe that God is somehow neutral concerning deviant sexual behavior are self-deceived and deluded. If the "wrath of God is revealed from heaven" against such behavior, that means that it is indeed sin.

UNCLEANNESS (AKATHARSIA)

Always translated as uncleanness, **akatharsia** means either physical or moral impurity.[3] It appears to be oriented to lifestyle. In the Old Testament, uncleanness was associated with either a medical condition involving a blood issue, such as female menstruation, or a disease such as leprosy. The Greek term appears to be related to riotous living that would be conducive to sexually transmitted diseases. References include:

> 19 I speak after the manner of men because of the infirmity of your flesh: for as ye have yielded your members servants to uncleanness and to iniquity unto iniquity; even so now yield your members servants to righteousness unto holiness. ROMANS 6:19 (KJV)

> 21 And lest, when I come again, my God will humble me among you, and that I shall bewail many which have sinned already, and have not repented of the uncleanness and fornication and lasciviousness which they have committed. 2 CORINTHIANS 12:21 (KJV)

Uncleanness is generally associated with sexual immorality.

LASCIVIOUSNESS (ASELGEIA)

Lasciviousness (**aselgeia**) is associated with wantonness. Strong's describes it as unbridled lust, excess, licentiousness, lasciviousness, wantonness, outrageousness, shamelessness, and insolence.[4] Lasciviousness shocks public decency. This would be in line with the Lesbian, Gay, Bisexual,

Transgender, Questioning (LBGTQ) Coalition that is plaguing public schools, colleges, and public institutions. This would include gender neutral restrooms, bathing facilities, dormitories, etc. As with uncleanness, lasciviousness is associated with all manner of sexual immorality. Vine's explanation is as follows:[5]

LASCIVIOUS, LASCIVIOUSNESS

aselgeia (ἀσέλγεια, 766) denotes "excess, licentiousness, absence of restraint, indecency, wantonness"; "lasciviousness" in Mark 7:22, one of the evils that proceed from the heart; in 2 Cor. 12:21, one of the evils of which some in the church at Corinth had been guilty; in Gal. 5:19, classed among the works of the flesh; in Eph. 4:19, among the sins of the unregenerate who are "past feeling"; so in 1 Pet. 4:3; in Jude 4, of that into which the grace of God had been turned by ungodly men; it is translated "wantonness" in Rom. 13:13, one of the sins against which believers are warned; in 2 Pet. 2:2, according to the best mss., "lascivious (doings)," rv(the kjv"pernicious ways" follows those texts which have apoleiais); in v. 7, rv, "lascivious (life)," kjv, "filthy (conversation)," of the people of Sodom and Gomorrah; in 2:18, rv, "lasciviousness" (kjv, "wantonness"), practiced by the same persons as mentioned in Jude. The prominent idea is shameless conduct. Some have derived the word from a, negative, and selge, "a city in Pisidia." Others, with similar improbability, trace it to a, negative, and selgo, or thelgo, "to charm." See wantonness.

---

17 This I say therefore, and testify in the Lord, that ye henceforth walk not as other Gentiles walk, in the vanity of their mind, 18 Having the understanding darkened, being alienated from the life of God through the ignorance that is in them, because of the blindness of their heart: 19 Who being past feeling have given themselves over unto lasciviousness, to work all uncleanness with greediness. EPHESIANS 4:17-19 (KJV)

3 For the time past of our life may suffice us to have wrought the will of the Gentiles, when we walked in lasciviousness, lusts, excess of wine, revellings, banquetings, and abominable idolatries: 4 Wherein they think it strange that ye run not with them to the same excess of riot, speaking evil of you: 1 PETER 4:3-4 (KJV)

IDOLATRY (EIDNLOLATRIA)

Most people associate idolatry with the worship of sticks and stones formed into some sort of image of man, animals, plants, or monsters. Worshipping the creature rather than the Creator God, who is eternal, is something that goes back to almost the beginning of man. According to Romans 1, this is also the product of a reprobate mind. The idol being the object of worship, Vine defines "idol"[6] as:

IDOL

eidolon (εἴδωλον, 1497), primarily "a phantom or likeness" (from eidos, "an appearance," lit., "that which is seen"), or "an idea, fancy," denotes in the NT (a) "an idol," an image to represent a false god, Acts 7:41; 1 Cor. 12:2; Rev. 9:20; (b) "the false god" worshipped in an image, Acts 15:20; Rom. 2:22; 1 Cor. 8:4, 7; 10:19; 2 Cor. 6:16; 1 Thess. 1:9; 1 John 5:21. "The corresponding Heb. word denotes 'vanity,' Jer. 14:22; 18:15; 'thing of nought,' Lev. 19:4, marg., cf. Eph. 4:17. Hence what represented a deity to the Gentiles, was to Paul a 'vain thing,' Acts 14:15; 'nothing in the world,' 1 Cor. 8:4; 10:19. Jeremiah calls the idol a 'scarecrow' ('pillar in a garden,' 10:5, marg.), and Isaiah, 44:9-20, etc., and Habakkuk, 2:18, 19 and the Psalmist, 115:4-8, etc., are all equally scathing. It is important to notice, however, that in each case the people of God are addressed. When he speaks to idolaters, Paul, knowing that no man is won by ridicule, adopts a different line, Acts 14:15-18; 17:16, 21-31."

There is a secondary New Testament meaning:

5 Mortify therefore your members which are upon the earth; fornication, uncleanness, inordinate affection, evil concupiscence, and covetousness, which is idolatry: COLOSSIANS 3:5 (KJV)

Idolatry associated with covetousness would indicate that anything held above God is an idol. We are warned to stay away from such things.

12 Wherefore, my dearly beloved, flee from idolatry. 1 CORINTHIANS 10:12 (KJV)

Many things are held above God, such as evolutionary science, the love of money, and a love of activities like sports that compete with time taken for spiritual things. Basically, the love of the things of this world to the exclusion of God is idolatry.

WITCHCRAFT (PHARMAKEIA)

Pharmakeia is the Greek work from which we get "pharmacy" and "pharmaceutical." It should not be surprising that the word translated as "witchcraft" has to do with the illicit use of drugs. This may or may not be specifically in the realm of sorcery and prognostication.[7] The modern equivalent would be hallucinogenic drugs such as LSD, mescaline, acylimine mushrooms, PCP, or marijuana; pain killers such as morphine-based drugs; drugs used to make one feel superhuman such as methamphetamine or cocaine; or mood-altering drugs, such as those prescribed for hyperactivity or depression. The fact that many of these drugs are by prescription only does not change the fact that taking them constitutes a Work of the Flesh. The word is only used three times in the New Testament, with the other two translated as "sorceries." Both are found in the Book of Revelation as things not repented of.

21 Neither repented they of their murders, nor of their sorceries, nor of their fornication, nor of their thefts. REVELATION 9:21 (KJV)

The second Revelation reference describes Babylon falling.

23 And the light of a candle shall shine no more at all in thee; and the voice of the bridegroom and of the bride shall be heard no more at all in thee: for thy merchants were the great men of the earth; for by thy sorceries were all nations deceived. REVELATION 18:23 (KJV)

None should think that the Bible is silent when it comes to the use of drugs.

HATRED (ECHTHRAI)

This is a word that is feminine in gender with a meaning of enmity.[8] It is normally used to describe the relationship between God and the World. Elsewhere, the normal translation is "enmity."

7 Because the carnal mind is enmity against God: for it is not subject to the law of God, neither indeed can be. ROMANS 8:7 (KJV)

15 Having abolished in his flesh the enmity, even the law of commandments contained in ordinances; for to make in himself of twain one new man, so making peace; 16 And that he might reconcile both unto God in one body by the cross, having slain the enmity thereby: EPHESIANS 2:15-16 (KJV)

4 Ye adulterers and adulteresses, know ye not that the friendship of the world is enmity with God? whosoever therefore will be a friend of the world is the enemy of God. JAMES 4:4 (KJV)

Hatred, in this case, leans foremost towards a hatred of God.

VARIANCE (ERIS)

A synonym for this could be "contentious," but is often translated as "strife."[9] There are times when we are admonished to be contentious.

> *3 Beloved, when I gave all diligence to write unto you of the common salvation, it was needful for me to write unto you, and exhort you that ye should earnestly contend for the faith which was once delivered unto the saints. JUDE 1:3 (KJV)*

There are times when we must speak out as faithful Christians on behalf of God and His Word. The Work of the Flesh means to be quarrelsome.

> *13 Let us walk honestly, as in the day; not in rioting and drunkenness, not in chambering and wantonness, not in strife and envying. ROMANS 13:13 (KJV)*

> *11 For it hath been declared unto me of you, my brethren, by them which are of the house of Chloe, that there are contentions among you. 1 CORINTHIANS 1:11 (KJV)*

A Christian should not wade into an argument for the argument's sake. We are, however, to be bold in proclaiming the Gospel:

> *18 Praying always with all prayer and supplication in the Spirit, and watching thereunto with all perseverance and supplication for all saints; 19 And for me, that utterance may be given unto me, that I may open my mouth boldly, to make known the mystery of the gospel, 20 For which I am an ambassador in bonds: that therein I may speak boldly, as I ought to speak. EPHESIANS 6:18-20 (KJV)*

We are to be bold, but respectful.

15 But sanctify the Lord God in your hearts: and be ready always to give an answer to every man that asketh you a reason of the hope that is in you with meekness and fear: 1 PETER 3:15 (KJV)

EMULATIONS (ZELOS)

This is another word with good and bad connotation. It can mean to passionately intervene for someone else, or for a cause. It can also mean an envious, contentious, or jealous rivalry.[10] On the good side, it is written of Jesus and translated as "zeal":

13 And the Jews' passover was at hand, and Jesus went up to Jerusalem, 14 And found in the temple those that sold oxen and sheep and doves, and the changers of money sitting: 15 And when he had made a scourge of small cords, he drove them all out of the temple, and the sheep, and the oxen; and poured out the changers' money, and overthrew the tables; 16 And said unto them that sold doves, Take these things hence; make not my Father's house an house of merchandise. 17 And his disciples remembered that it was written, The zeal of thine house hath eaten me up. JOHN 2:13-17 (KJV)

It is also written of Israel and translated as "zeal":

1 Brethren, my heart's desire and prayer to God for Israel is, that they might be saved. 2 For I bear them record that they have a zeal of God, but not according to knowledge. ROMANS 10:1-2 (KJV)

And of the Apostle Paul and translated as "jealous":

2 For I am jealous over you with godly jealousy: for I have espoused you to one husband, that I may present you as a chaste virgin to Christ. 2 CORINTHIANS 11:2 (KJV)

A similar word in the verb form, translated as "zealous,"[11] is used of believers:

14 Who gave himself for us, that he might redeem us from all iniquity, and purify unto himself a peculiar people, zealous of good works. TITUS 2:14 (KJV)

On the bad side, **zelos** is translated as "indignation," "envy," and "envying." What is displayed is selfish passions.

17 Then the high priest rose up, and all they that were with him, (which is the sect of the Sadducees,) and were filled with indignation, 18 And laid their hands on the apostles, and put them in the common prison. ACTS 5:17-18 (KJV)

45 But when the Jews saw the multitudes, they were filled with envy, and spake against those things which were spoken by Paul, contradicting and blaspheming. ACTS 13:45 (KJV)

3 For ye are yet carnal: for whereas there is among you envying, and strife, and divisions, are ye not carnal, and walk as men? 1 CORINTHIANS 3:3 (KJV)

The difference between good and evil appears to be in where passion is directed, either for the betterment of others, or towards the justification of selfish actions.

WRATH (THUMOI)

According to Strong, **thumoi** means a passionate, explosive anger, as opposed to pent-up feelings.[12] It is like a pot that rapidly boils over and then subsides. Luke gives us a sense of the term in the account of Jesus speaking in the synagogue in His own hometown of Nazareth. Because He made His claim as Messiah, they were ready and eager to stone him.

> 28 And all they in the synagogue, when they heard these things, were filled with wrath, 29 And rose up, and thrust him out of the city, and led him unto the brow of the hill whereon their city was built, that they might cast him down headlong. LUKE 4:28-29 (KJV)

Another account of an angry mob is found in the book of Acts. A silversmith of Ephesus named Demetrius works up his trade union to high emotion concerning their trade of making images of Dianna. After Paul brought the Gospel to the city, their business started dropping off and their livelihood was threatened. This made the whole crowd very angry.

> 28 And when they heard these sayings, they were full of wrath, and cried out, saying, Great is Diana of the Ephesians. 29 And the whole city was filled with confusion: and having caught Gaius and Aristarchus, men of Macedonia, Paul's companions in travel, they rushed with one accord into the theatre. ACTS 19:28-29 (KJV)

It is evident that the group had some mischief in mind for these two individuals. The riot lasted for several hours. The "wrath" spoken of in these passages is a wrath of action and substance. It is not mere disagreement.

STRIFE (ERITHEIAI)

Variance and strife are very closely related in meaning. This word, however, has no good side to it. It is selfish partisanship, wrangling, or factiousness.[13] It is generally translated as "strife." It is sometimes used to describe a selfish action stemming from jealousy.

> 15 Some indeed preach Christ even of envy and strife; and some also of good will: 16 The one preach Christ of contention, not sincerely, supposing to add affliction to my bonds: 17 But the other of love, knowing that I am set for the defense of the gospel. PHILIPPIANS 1:15-17 (KJV)

It is used of those trying to gain superiority.

> 3 Let nothing be done through strife or vainglory; but in lowliness of mind let each esteem other better than themselves. PHILIPPIANS 2:3 (KJV)

It is also used with "envying" to describe those who use subversion to gain position.

> 13 Who is a wise man and endued with knowledge among you? let him shew out of a good conversation his works with meekness of wisdom. 14 But if ye have bitter envying and strife in your hearts, glory not, and lie not against the truth. 15 This wisdom descendeth not from above, but is earthly, sensual, devilish. 16 For where envying and strife is, there is confusion and every evil work. JAMES 3:13-16 (KJV)

This type of "strife" is associated with those trying to gain an advantage within a group. It is best described as political tactics.

SEDITIONS (DICHOSTASIA)

Dichostasia defined as dissension or division.[14] The only passage where this word is used outside of a listing of Works of the Flesh it is translated as "divisions."

> 17 Now I beseech you, brethren, mark them which cause divisions and offences contrary to the doctrine which ye have learned; and avoid them. ROMANS 16:11 (KJV)

Though we know little about this term, it is evident that it is division caused by the promotion of doctrinal error. The remedy is to avoid the error by avoiding the individual.

HERESIES (HAIRESEIS)

Haireseis is generally associated with divisions or sectarianism, however the word itself means "to choose."[15] The idea of a sect is borne out by the use of the word translated as "sect" in various places in the Gospel accounts:

> 17 Then the high priest rose up, and all they that were with him, (which is the sect of the Sadducees,) and were filled with indignation, ACTS 5:15 (KJV)

> 5 But there rose up certain of the sect of the Pharisees which believed, saying, That it was needful to circumcise them, and to command them to keep the law of Moses. ACTS 5:5 (KJV)

> 5 For we have found this man a pestilent fellow, and a mover of sedition among all the Jews throughout the world, and a ringleader of the sect of the Nazarenes: ACTS 24:5 (KJV)

Heresy is defined by Vine as follows:

> *hairesis (airesis) denotes (a) "a choosing, choice"(from haireomai, "to choose"); then, "that which is chosen," and hence, "an opinion," especially a self-willed opinion, which is substituted for submission to the power of truth, and leads to division and the formation of sects, Gal. 5:20 (marg., "parties"); such erroneous opinions are frequently the outcome of personal preference or the prospect of advantage; see 2 Pet. 2:1, where "destructive" (R.V.) signifies leading to ruin; some assign even this to (b); in the papyri the prevalent meaning is "choice" (Moulton and Milligan, Vocab.); (b) a sect; this secondary meaning, resulting from (a), is the dominating significance in the N.T., Acts 5:17; 15:5; 24:5,14; 26:5; 28:22; "heresies" in I Cor. 11:19 (se marg.). See Sect.*[16]

Vine also addresses the confusion in interpretation and gives further explanation concerning the term "sect."

> *hairesis (airesis) "a choosing," is translated "sect" throughout the Acts, except in 24:14, K.J.V., "heresy" (R.V. "sect"); it properly denotes a predilection either for a particular truth, or for a perversion of one, generally with the expectation of personal advantage; hence, a division and the formation of a party or "sect" in contrast to the uniting power of "the truth," held in toto; "a sect" is a division developed and brought to an issue; the order "divisions, heresies" (marg. "parties") in "the works of the flesh" in Gal. 5:19-21 is suggestive of this. See Heresy.*[17]

The use of the term heresy in the Scriptures is generally associated with those who hold doctrines apart from the truth of the Word of God. Instead, they pervert the truth and choose to interpret it in a fashion that is more convenient to themselves. This more convenient lie gives rise to factions and sectarianism. The term is specifically used concerning false teachers.

1 But there were false prophets also among the people, even as there shall be false teachers among you, who privily shall bring in damnable heresies, even denying the Lord that bought them, and bring upon themselves swift destruction. 2 PETER 2:1 (KJV)

Heretics are true destroyers of the faith with false gospels, varying notions of sin, corruption of doctrine, and the promotion of works contrary to the truth. More than that, it is the promotion of selfish choices that are made in avoidance of the truth. Modern decision-making models would fit this criterion. They include the promotion of "values clarification," "dialectics," and any multi-step model for making moral decisions, such as used in Alcoholics Anonymous, that is not based on the sound teachings of Scripture.

ENVYINGS (PHTHOVOU)

This word is always translated as "envy" or "envyings."[18] A synonym may be "jealousy," usually with mischievous intent.

17 Therefore when they were gathered together, Pilate said unto them, Whom will ye that I release unto you? Barabbas, or Jesus which is called Christ? 18 For he knew that for envy they had delivered him. MATTHEW 27:17-18 (KJV)

8 And the multitude crying aloud began to desire him to do as he had ever done unto them. 9 But Pilate answered them, saying, Will ye that I release unto you the King of the Jews? 10 For he knew that the chief priests had delivered him for envy. MARK 15:8-10 (KJV)

The remainder of the references are primarily listings of Works of the Flesh, with one exception.

4 Ye adulterers and adulteresses, know ye not that the friendship of the world is enmity with God? whosoever therefore will be a friend of the world is the enemy of God. 5 -- Do ye think that the scripture saith in vain, The spirit that dwelleth in us lusteth to envy? JAMES 4:4-5 (KJV)

The Spirit of God has an envy that would exclude anything that is not Holy. The Lord is jealous of our love of the world, and it is described as mutually exclusive. Envy, therefore, has only one object of satisfaction, with anything else meeting disapproval.

MURDERS (PHONOI)

Phonos is primarily translated as "murder," but is also translated as "slaughter."[19] The example of Scripture implies the malicious and unlawful taking of human life.

7 And there was one named Barabbas, which lay bound with them that had made insurrection with him, who had committed murder in the insurrection. MARK 15:7 (KJV)

The following passage translates the word as "slaughter" in describing the persecution led by Saul (afterword known as the Apostle Paul).

1 And Saul, yet breathing out threatenings and slaughter against the disciples of the Lord, went unto the high priest, ACTS 9:1 (KJV)

We are confronted more in these last days with all forms of murder than we have been in many centuries. Dictators have starved their citizens in Ukraine and China, the Jews were largely slaughtered by Adolf Hitler, radical Islam first slaughtered thousands of Armenian Christians under the Ottoman Empire and now, under ISIS, many more Christians are murdered, and here in America we have killed over fifty million babies with abortion. It is apparent that murder is a justifiable sin all around the world. In the case of babies, it is even used as a form of birth control. Now we are moving deeper into senselessness with the killing of babies already born (infanticide), killing the old and infirmed (euthanasia), and killing of self (suicide). All of these things are becoming legal and are encouraged.

DRUNKENNESS (METHAI)

Drunkenness is defined as "intoxication," and in most states and Europe that is a statutory 0.08% blood alcohol level.[20] Culturally, the Nation of Israel drank a great deal of wine. Our Lord's first miracle was to turn water into wine at the Wedding Feast of Cana.

1 And the third day there was a marriage in Cana of Galilee; and the mother of Jesus was there: 2 And both Jesus was called, and his disciples, to the marriage. 3 And when they wanted wine, the mother of Jesus saith unto him, They have no wine. 4 Jesus saith unto her, Woman, what have I to do with thee? mine hour is not yet come. 5 His mother saith unto the servants, Whatsoever he saith unto you, do it. 6 And there were set there six waterpots of stone, after the manner of the purifying of the Jews, containing two or three firkins apiece. 7 Jesus saith unto them, Fill the waterpots with water. And they filled them up to the brim. 8 And he saith unto them, Draw out now, and bear unto the governor of the feast. And they bare it. 9 -- When the ruler of the feast had tasted the water that was made wine, and knew not whence it was: (but the servants which drew the water knew;) the governor of the feast called the bridegroom, 10 And saith unto him, Every man at the beginning doth set forth good wine; and when men have well drunk, then that which is worse: but thou hast kept the good wine until now. JOHN 2:1-10 (KJV)

It is evident from what the caterer said about the wine that it was good aged wine. The Jewish Sadr, also known as the Feast of Unleavened Bread, has four cups of wine associated with it. This Feast was where the Lord's Table was instituted. We see two of these cups presented in the Luke account: one during the meal in verse 17, and one after the meal in verse 20.

> *13 And they went, and found as he had said unto them: and they made ready the passover. 14 And when the hour was come, he sat down, and the twelve apostles with him. 15 And he said unto them, With desire I have desired to eat this passover with you before I suffer: 16 For I say unto you, I will not any more eat thereof, until it be fulfilled in the kingdom of God. 17 And he took the cup, and gave thanks, and said, Take this, and divide it among yourselves: 18 For I say unto you, I will not drink of the fruit of the vine, until the kingdom of God shall come.*

> *19 And he took bread, and gave thanks, and brake it, and gave unto them, saying, This is my body which is given for you: this do in remembrance of me. 20 Likewise also the cup after supper, saying, This cup is the new testament in my blood, which is shed for you. LUKE 22:13-20 (KJV)*

Jesus also used fermentation as an example.

> *22 And no man putteth new wine into old bottles: else the new wine doth burst the bottles, and the wine is spilled, and the bottles will be marred: but new wine must be put into new bottles. MARK 2:22 (KJV)*

Finally, we see the Apostle Paul telling Timothy that wine may have some medicinal value.

23 Drink no longer water, but use a little wine for thy stomach's sake and thine often infirmities. 1 TIMOTHY 5:23 (KJV)

There are those in Christian circles who insist that the wine of the Bible is non-alcoholic grape juice, but this hardly fits what the Bible has to say about the drink. The wine of the Bible is made from fermented grapes.

If the Nation of Israel was so obsessed with drinking wine, and if our Lord participated in this as having a proper social life, then what constitutes "drunkenness"? The New Testament does give guidance.

18 And be not drunk with wine, wherein is excess; but be filled with the Spirit; EPHESIANS 5:18 (KJV)

It is a question of controlling influence. We are to walk by the Spirit, and the Lord is to be the controlling influence in our lives. If any substance has control of your life, then it is too much.

12 All things are lawful unto me, but all things are not expedient: all things are lawful for me, but I will not be brought under the power of any. 13 Meats for the belly, and the belly for meats: but God shall destroy both it and them. Now the body is not for fornication, but for the Lord; and the Lord for the body. 1 CORINTHIANS 6:12-13 (KJV)

We should therefore not condemn the abstainer nor the moderate drinker, but those who are controlled by any substance are not in control of themselves, nor are they controlled by the Spirit of God. This is why instructions for choosing Church leadership includes a requirement concerning their drinking habits. Of a Bishop or Overseer, it is written:

2 A bishop then must be blameless, the husband of one wife, vigilant, sober, of good behaviour, given to hospitality, apt to teach; 3 Not given to wine, no striker, not greedy of filthy lucre; but patient, not a brawler, not covetous; 1 TIMOTHY 3:2-3 (KJV)

7 For a bishop must be blameless, as the steward of God; not selfwilled, not soon angry, not given to wine, no striker, not given to filthy lucre; TITUS 1:7 (KJV)

Of a Deacon it is also written:

8 Likewise must the deacons be grave, not doubletongued, not given to much wine, not greedy of filthy lucre; 1 TIMOTHY 3:8 (KJV)

Notice that wine is not forbidden, but it is limited. The aged believers are also admonished to limit their alcoholic intake.

2 That the aged men be sober, grave, temperate, sound in faith, in charity, in patience. 3 The aged women likewise, that they be in behaviour as becometh holiness, not false accusers, not given to much wine, teachers of good things; TITUS 2:2-3 (KJV)

There is a reason given to abstain from alcoholic beverages, but it is not for legalistic purposes. It is for the conscience of the weaker brother.

19 Let us therefore follow after the things which make for peace, and things wherewith one may edify another. 20 For meat destroy not the work of God. All things indeed are pure; but it is evil for that man who eateth with offence. 21 It is good neither to eat flesh, nor to drink wine, nor any thing whereby thy brother stumbleth, or is offended, or is made weak. 22 Hast thou faith? have it to thyself before God. Happy is he that condemneth not himself in that thing which he alloweth. 23 And he that doubteth is damned if he eat, because he eateth not of faith: for whatsoever is not of faith is sin. ROMANS 14:19-23 (KJV)

If you have a brother who is weak through the flesh concerning alcohol, it is best for his sake to abstain from its use. More will be said about the conscience in the next chapter, but anything that hinders the struggle of another to overcome their fleshly addictions should be avoided. If we know someone who has a drinking problem, our example to them means a great deal. We should never add to the temptation of another.

With stronger drink more readily available, such as whiskey, gin, tequila, and rum, the excuse of drinking gets harder to justify. It is no longer something done to be sociable. It is drinking for the effect alcohol gives. The intentional use of substances for effect in a party atmosphere is called "reveling."

REVELING (KAMOI)

Kamoi is defined in Strong as follows:

> *A nocturnal and riotous procession of half drunken and frolicsome fellows who after supper parade through the streets with torches and music in honor of Bacchus or some other deity, and sing and play before houses of male and female friends; hence used generally of feasts and drinking parties that are protracted till late at night and indulge in revelry.*[21]

Examples in Scripture are limited. The term is used only three times in the New Testament, translated twice as "reveling" and once as "rioting." Those who engage in such behavior could be described as "party animals."

13 Let us walk honestly, as in the day; not in rioting and drunkenness, not in chambering and wantonness, not in strife and envying. 14 But put ye on the Lord Jesus Christ, and make not provision for the flesh, to fulfil the lusts thereof. ROMANS 13:13-14 (KJV)

1 Forasmuch then as Christ hath suffered for us in the flesh, arm yourselves likewise with the same mind: for he that hath suffered in the flesh hath ceased from sin; 2 That he no longer should live the rest of his time in the flesh to the lusts of men, but to the will of God. 3 For the time past of our life may suffice us to have wrought the will of the Gentiles, when we walked in lasciviousness, lusts, excess of wine, revellings, banquetings, and abominable idolatries: 4 Wherein they think it strange that ye run not with them to the same excess of riot, speaking evil of you: 1 PETER 4:1-4 (KJV)

Such reveling is worldliness. If we belong to Christ, we no longer belong to the degradations of this world.

THE LIKE THINGS

"Like things" are the Works of the Flesh mentioned elsewhere in the Bible. Many of these are tabulated in the table on the following pages. There are nearly 130 references, with approximately thirty duplicate Works of the Flesh and several more that are similar. Unfortunately, the list is not exhaustive. Tabulated are the translation, Strong's number, Greek pneumonic, and the Scripture location where it was found.

Some of these sins appear to be more serious than others, but all are sinful to God. There is not a single sin that has not been paid for by the Lord on Calvary's Cross.

8 But God commendeth his love toward us, in that, while we were yet sinners, Christ died for us. ROMANS 5:8 (KJV)

Apart from the controlling power of the Holy Spirit of God, there is nothing on that list that any of us is not capable of doing. If we are caught up in any Work of the Flesh, the remedy is the same for all

5 This then is the message which we have heard of him, and declare unto you, that God is light, and in him is no darkness at all. 6 If we say that we have fellowship with him, and walk in darkness, we lie, and do not the truth: 7 But if we walk in the light, as he is in the light, we have fellowship one with another, and the blood of Jesus Christ his Son cleanseth us from all sin.

8 If we say that we have no sin, we deceive ourselves, and the truth is not in us. 9 If we confess our sins, he is faithful and just to forgive us our sins, and to cleanse us from all unrighteousness. 10 If we say that we have not sinned, we make him a liar, and his word is not in us. 1 JOHN 1:5-10 (KJV)

WORKS OF THE FLESH

WORK OF THE FLESH	STRONG'S #	GREEK PNEUMONIC	SCRIPTURE
vile affections	g3806, g0819	pathos atimias	Romans 1:26
fornication	g4202	porneia	Romans 1:29
wickedness	g4189	poneria	Romans 1:29
covetousness	g4124	pleonexia	Romans 1:29
maliciousness	g2549	kakia	Romans 1:29
envy	g5355	phthonos	Romans 1:29
murders	g5408	phonos	Romans 1:29
debate	g2054	eris	Romans 1:29
deceit	g1388	dolos	Romans 1:29
malignity	g2550	kakoetheia	Romans 1:29
whisperers	g5588	psithyristes	Romans 1:29
backbiters	g2637	katalalos	Romans 1:30
God haters	g2319	theostyges	Romans 1:30
insolent	g5197	hybristes	Romans 1:30
arrogant	g5244	hyperephanos	Romans 1:30
disobedient to parents	g0545, g1118	apeithes gonens	Romans 1:30
boaster	g0123	alazon	Romans 1:30
inventors of evil things	g2182, g2556	epheuretēs kakos	Romans 1:30
without understanding	g0801	asynetos	Romans 1:31
covenant breakers	g0802	asynthetos	Romans 1:31
without natural affection	g0794	astorgos	Romans 1:31
implacable	g0786	aspondos	Romans 1:31
unmerciful	g0415	aneleemon	Romans 1:31
rioting	g2970	komos	Romans 13:13
drunkenness	g3178	methai	Romans 13:13
chambering	g2845	koitē	Romans 13:13
wantonness	g0766	aselgeia	Romans 13:13

WORKS OF THE FLESH (CONTINUED)

WORK OF THE FLESH	STRONG'S #	GREEK PNEUMONIC	SCRIPTURE
strife	g2054	eris	Romans 13:13
envying	g2205	zelos	Romans 13:13
adultery	g3430	moicheia	Galatians 5:19
fornication	g4202	porneia	Galatians 5:19
uncleanness	g0167	akatharsia	Galatians 5:19
lasciviousness	g0766	aselgeia	Galatians 5:19
idolatry	g1497	eidolon	Galatians 5:20
witchcraft	g5331	pharmakia	Galatians 5:20
hatred	g2189	echtha	Galatians 5:20
variance	g2054	eris	Galatians 5:20
emulations	g2205	zelos	Galatians 5:20
wrath	g2372	thumoi	Galatians 5:20
strife	g2052	eritheiai	Galatians 5:20
seditions	g1370	dichostasia	Galatians 5:20
heresies	g0139	haireseis	Galatians 5:20
envying	g5355	phthovou	Galatians 5:21
murders	g5408	phonoi	Galatians 5:21
drunkenness	g3178	methai	Galatians 5:21
reveling	g2970	kamoi	Galatians 5:21
bitterness	g4088	pikria	Ephesians 4:31
wrath	g2372	thymos	Ephesians 4:31
anger	g3709	orgē	Ephesians 4:31
clamor	g2906	kraugē	Ephesians 4:31
evil speaking	g0988	blasphēmia	Ephesians 4:31
filthiness	g0151	aischrotēs	Ephesians 5:4
foolish talking	g3473	mōrologia	Ephesians 5:4
jesting	g2160	eutrapelia	Ephesians 5:4
whoremonger	g4205	pornos	Ephesians 5:5
uncleanness	g0169	akathartos	Ephesians 5:5
covetousness	g4123	pleonektēs	Ephesians 5:5

WORKS OF THE FLESH (CONTINUED)

WORK OF THE FLESH	STRONG'S #	GREEK PNEUMONIC	SCRIPTURE
idolatry	g1497	eidōlolatrēs	Ephesians 5:5
anger	g3709	orgē	Colossians 3:8
wrath	g2372	thymos	Colossians 3:8
malice	g2549	kakia	Colossians 3:8
blasphemy	g0988	blasphēmia	Colossians 3:8
filthy communication	g0148	aischrologia	Colossians 3:8
lawless	g0459	anomos	1 Timothy 1:9
disobedient	g0506	anypotaktos	1 Timothy 1:9
ungodly	g0765	asebēs	1 Timothy 1:9
sinners	g0268	hamartōlos	1 Timothy 1:9
unholy	g0462	anosios	1 Timothy 1:9
profane	g0952	bebēlos	1 Timothy 1:9
murders of fathers	g3964	patrolōas	1 Timothy 1:9
murders of mothers	g3389	mētrolōas	1 Timothy 1:9
manslayers	g0409	androphonos	1 Timothy 1:9
whoremonger	g4205	pornos	1 Timothy 1:10
defilers of self	g0733	arsenokoitēs	1 Timothy 1:10
men stealers	g0405	andrapodistēs	1 Timothy 1:10
liars	g5583	pseustēs	1 Timothy 1:10
perjured persons	g1965	epiorkos	1 Timothy 1:10
self-lovers	g5367	philautos	2 Timothy 3:2
covetousness	g5366	philargyros	2 Timothy 3:2
boaster	g0213	alazōn	2 Timothy 3:2
proud	g5244	hyperēphanos	2 Timothy 3:2
blasphemy	g0989	blasphēmos	2 Timothy 3:2
disobedient to parents	g0545, g1118	apeithes gonens	2 Timothy 3:2
unthankful	g0884	acharistos	2 Timothy 3:2
unholy	g0462	anosios	2 Timothy 3:2

WORKS OF THE FLESH (CONTINUED)

WORK OF THE FLESH	STRONG'S #	GREEK PNEUMONIC	SCRIPTURE
without natural affection	g0794	astorgos	2 Timothy 3:3
trucebreakers	g0786	aspondos	2 Timothy 3:3
false accusers	g1228	diabolos	2 Timothy 3:3
incontinent	g0193	akratēs	2 Timothy 3:3
fierce	g0434	anēmeros	2 Timothy 3:3
haters of good men	g0865	aphilagathos	2 Timothy 3:3
traitors	g4273	prodotēs	2 Timothy 3:4
heady	g4312	propetēs	2 Timothy 3:4
high minded	g5187	typhoō	2 Timothy 3:4
pleasure lovers	g5369	philēdonos	2 Timothy 3:4
disobedient	g0545	apeithēs	Titus 3:3
deceived	g4105	planaō	Titus 3:3
lusts	g1939	epithymia	Titus 3:3
pleasures	g2237	hēdonē	Titus 3:3
malice	g2549	kakia	Titus 3:3
envy	g5355	phthono	Titus 3:3
hateful	g4767	stygnētos	Titus 3:3
licentiousness	g0766	aselgeia	1 Peter 4:3
lusts	g1939	epithymia	1 Peter 4:3
excess of wine	g3632	oinophlygia	1 Peter 4:3
reveling	g2970	kōmos	1 Peter 4:3
banqueting	g4224	potos	1 Peter 4:3
idolatry	g1495	eidōlolatreia	1 Peter 4:3
rioting	g0810	asōtia	1 Peter 4:4
evil speaking	g0987	blasphēmeō	1 Peter 4:4
wicked	g0113	athesmos	2 Peter 2:7
filthy conversation	g0766, g0391	aselgeia anastrophē	2 Peter 2:7
lusts	g1939	epithymia	2 Peter 2:10

WORKS OF THE FLESH (CONTINUED)

WORK OF THE FLESH	STRONG'S #	GREEK PNEUMONIC	SCRIPTURE
uncleanness	g3394	*miasmos*	2 Peter 2:10
despisers of government	g2963 g2706	*kyriotēs kataphroneō*	2 Peter 2:10
presumptuous	g5113	*tolmētēs*	2 Peter 2:10
selfwilled	g0829	*authadēs*	2 Peter 2:10
evil speaking	g0987	*blasphēmeō*	2 Peter 2:10
rioting	g5172	*tryphē*	2 Peter 2:13
deceivings	g0539	*apatē*	2 Peter 2:13
adultery	g3428	*moichalis*	2 Peter 2:14
beguiling	g1185	*deleazō*	2 Peter 2:14
covetousness	g4124	*pleonexia*	2 Peter 2:14
murmuring	g1113	*goggystēs*	Jude 16
complaining	g3202	*mempsimoiros*	Jude 16
lustful	g1939	*epithymia*	Jude 16
making separations	g0592	*apodiorizō*	Jude 19
sensual	g5591	*psychikos*	Jude 19

CHAPTER EIGHT

FAITH, WORKS, AND SINS OF CONSCIENCE

IN CHAPTER 7, THE WORKS OF THE FLESH were examined in some detail. These are obvious sins, declared by God to be wrong in themselves. In this chapter, obligations and responsibilities of the believer viewed from the standpoint of faith, sin, and the expectations of God. Also examined are what could be termed sins of conscience. These are actions that cannot be taken by faith. Before any of this can be addressed, faith and its relationship to works must be explored. Since we are not righteous in ourselves, there is no amount of works that could commend us to God. However, God does have expectations for our behavior. Therefore, we must gain a better understanding of our faith and the works resulting from that faith.

FAITH AND WORKS

In Chapter 2, we examined Ephesians 2:8-10 from the standpoint of our present work of salvation. Now we need to look at the same passage from the standpoint of faith and works.

> *8 For by grace are ye saved through faith; and that not of yourselves: it is the gift of God: 9 Not of works, lest any man should boast. 10 For we are his workmanship, created in Christ Jesus unto good works, which God hath before ordained that we should walk in them. EPHESIANS 2:8-10 (KJV)*

The results of our ongoing salvation are ongoing works that have been prepared for us by God. It is God who reorders our lives for His purposes, and this results in good works. Believers are not even conscious that this is happening. Though not about the Church Age, there is a passage describing the judgment of those left at the end of the Tribulation prior to entering the Kingdom. This passage illustrates man's lack of cognizant thought concerning the motivation of his deeds.

31 When the Son of man shall come in his glory, and all the holy angels with him, then shall he sit upon the throne of his glory: 32 And before him shall be gathered all nations: and he shall separate them one from another, as a shepherd divideth his sheep from the goats: 33 And he shall set the sheep on his right hand, but the goats on the left. 34 Then shall the King say unto them on his right hand, Come, ye blessed of my Father, inherit the kingdom prepared for you from the foundation of the world: 35 For I was an hungred, and ye gave me meat: I was thirsty, and ye gave me drink: I was a stranger, and ye took me in: 36 Naked, and ye clothed me: I was sick, and ye visited me: I was in prison, and ye came unto me. 37 Then shall the righteous answer him, saying, Lord, when saw we thee an hungred, and fed thee? or thirsty, and gave thee drink? 38 -- When saw we thee a stranger, and took thee in? or naked, and clothed thee? 39 -- Or when saw we thee sick, or in prison, and came unto thee? 40 And the King shall answer and say unto them, Verily I say unto you, Inasmuch as ye have done it unto one of the least of these my brethren, ye have done it unto me. 41 Then shall he say also unto them on the left hand, Depart from me, ye cursed, into everlasting fire, prepared for the devil and his angels: 42 For I was an hungred, and ye gave me no meat: I was thirsty, and ye gave me no drink: 43 I was a stranger, and ye took me not in: naked, and ye clothed me not: sick, and in prison, and ye visited me not. 44 Then shall they also answer him, saying, Lord, when saw we thee an

hungred, or athirst, or a stranger, or naked, or sick, or in prison, and did
not minister unto thee? 45 Then shall he answer them, saying, Verily I
say unto you, Inasmuch as ye did it not to one of the least of these, ye did
it not to me. 46 And these shall go away into everlasting punishment:
but the righteous into life eternal. MATTHEW 25:31-46 (KJV)

It is apparent that neither those who are saved nor those who are
not saved understood how their lives were ordered. Those who were
not saved may have had "good works," but they were not found to be
in Christ. Therefore, they were judged based on their own deeds as not
measuring up. Those who were saved were just as surprised at their reward
and asked when did they do those things for which they were rewarded.

The conscious effort on the believer's part is to make sure he is of the
Spirit and in fellowship with God. The result will be the power of God
working through him, whether or not he is conscious of that fact. This
is how we will be viewed at the Judgment Seat of Christ.

9 Wherefore we labour, that, whether present or absent, we may be accepted
of him. 10 For we must all appear before the judgment seat of Christ; that
every one may receive the things done in his body, according to that he
hath done, whether it be good or bad. 2 CORINTHIANS 5:9-10 (KJV)

The following passage looks at our relationship to the Lord as laborers
in accordance with His Master Plan.

9 For we are labourers together with God: ye are God's husbandry, ye are
God's building. 10 According to the grace of God which is given unto me,
as a wise masterbuilder, I have laid the foundation, and another buildeth
thereon. But let every man take heed how he buildeth thereupon. 11 For
other foundation can no man lay than that is laid, which is Jesus Christ. 12

Now if any man build upon this foundation gold, silver, precious stones, wood, hay, stubble; 13 Every man's work shall be made manifest: for the day shall declare it, because it shall be revealed by fire; and the fire shall try every man's work of what sort it is. 14 If any man's work abide which he hath built thereupon, he shall receive a reward. 15 If any man's work shall be burned, he shall suffer loss: but he himself shall be saved; yet so as by fire. 1 CORINTHIANS 3:9-15 (KJV)

When we take things into our own hands and work according to our own plans, even our successes are inferior and will be burned up. As we work in accordance with God's plan, we build with things that are not perishable and that will last for an eternity. Our losses are our own fault for going our own way.

OBLIGATIONS

Even though our works are appointed by God, many have abandoned one of the most important of these: our obligations to our parents.

1 Children, obey your parents in the Lord: for this is right. 2 Honour thy father and mother; (which is the first commandment with promise;) 3 That it may be well with thee, and thou mayest live long on the earth. EPHESIANS 6:1-3 (KJV)

This is a reiteration of the fifth commandment handed down by God to Moses on Mount Sinai. This is obviously something that is very important to God. There may be occasions when people are called to leave their parents behind for an assignment from God, such as missions, but while we are here, we still have responsibilities. The Lord Jesus also let it be known that you were not to use religious ceremony to escape such responsibilities.

9 And he said unto them, Full well ye reject the commandment of God, that ye may keep your own tradition. 10 For Moses said, Honour thy father and thy mother; and, Whoso curseth father or mother, let him die the death: 11 But ye say, If a man shall say to his father or mother, It is Corban, that is to say, a gift, by whatsoever thou mightest be profited by me; he shall be free. 12 And ye suffer him no more to do ought for his father or his mother; 13 Making the word of God of none effect through your tradition, which ye have delivered: and many such like things do ye. MARK 7:9-13 (KJV)

"Corban" may have a similar application in America today. The elderly are often shipped off to homes at government expense. If they have any wealth, the family will often try to shelter it so that the government benefits are not curtailed. Most people consider this to be good business. It is not as certain that the Lord sees it in the same way. Often the elderly are then forgotten until they die.

The New Testament does not stop at care for parents:

3 Honour widows that are widows indeed. 4 But if any widow have children or nephews, let them learn first to shew piety at home, and to requite their parents: for that is good and acceptable before God. 5 Now she that is a widow indeed, and desolate, trusteth in God, and continueth in supplications and prayers night and day. 6 But she that liveth in pleasure is dead while she liveth. 7 And these things give in charge, that they may be blameless. 1 TIMOTHY 5:3-7 (KJV)

We have an obligation to care for family and to make sure that others are not burdened with our responsibilities. In case some have missed the seriousness of this responsibility, the Apostle Paul gave it some clarity.

8 But if any provide not for his own, and specially for those of his own house, he hath denied the faith, and is worse than an infidel. 1 TIMOTHY 5:8 (KJV)

Christians also have an obligation to provide for themselves.

10 For even when we were with you, this we commanded you, that if any would not work, neither should he eat. 11 For we hear that there are some which walk among you disorderly, working not at all, but are busybodies. 12 Now them that are such we command and exhort by our Lord Jesus Christ, that with quietness they work, and eat their own bread. 2 THESSALONIANS 3:10-12 (KJV)

And having provided for self, we have an opportunity to provide for others.

27 Pure religion and undefiled before God and the Father is this, To visit the fatherless and widows in their affliction, and to keep himself unspotted from the world. JAMES 1:27 (KJV)

James makes an argument for doing good deeds by faith as directed by God.

14 What doth it profit, my brethren, though a man say he hath faith, and have not works? can faith save him? 15 If a brother or sister be naked, and destitute of daily food, 16 And one of you say unto them, Depart in peace, be ye warmed and filled; notwithstanding ye give them not those things which are needful to the body; what doth it profit? 17 Even so faith, if it hath not works, is dead, being alone.

18 Yea, a man may say, Thou hast faith, and I have works: shew me thy faith without thy works, and I will shew thee my faith by my works. 19 Thou believest that there is one God; thou doest well: the devils also believe, and tremble. 20 But wilt thou know, O vain man, that faith without works is dead? 21 Was not Abraham our father justified by works, when he had offered Isaac his son upon the altar? 22 Seest thou how faith wrought with his works, and by works was faith made perfect? 23 And the scripture was fulfilled which saith, Abraham believed God, and it was imputed unto him for righteousness: and he was called the Friend of God. 24 Ye see then how that by works a man is justified, and not by faith only.

25 Likewise also was not Rahab the harlot justified by works, when she had received the messengers, and had sent them out another way?

26 For as the body without the spirit is dead, so faith without works is dead also. JAMES 2:14-26 (KJV)

We are not made righteous before God by our works, but if we are the Lord's we will have good works. Good works are a result of faith in the finished work of Jesus Christ. They are not a cause in themselves.

SINS OF CONSCIENCE

In Chapter 2, it was recounted how man gained a conscience at his fall in the Garden of Eden. Prior to eating the fruit from the "Tree of the Knowledge of Good and Evil," we see in Genesis that they were innocent concerning any thought of sin.

25 And they were both naked, the man and his wife, and were not ashamed. GENESIS 2:25 (KJV)

After man's fall, we immediately read of his personal concern for sin.

7 And the eyes of them both were opened, and they knew that they were naked; and they sewed fig leaves together, and made themselves aprons. GENESIS 3:7 (KJV)

The newly developed conscience of man was imperfect and subject to change. There is very little said about the conscience in the Old Testament, but there is a great deal said about it in the New Testament. The conscience is where decisions are made concerning that which is good and that which is evil. If the conscience is not fully updated and informed by the Word of God, then it is subject to error. The believer is to live life by a good conscience, and warning is given to those who do not.

19 Holding faith, and a good conscience; which some having put away concerning faith have made shipwreck: 1 TIMOTHY 1:19 (KJV)

Believers are not only to protect their own conscience, but they are also to look after the conscience of other believers. Nowhere in the New Testament is this better explained than in the Apostle Paul's writings to the Corinthians concerning meat sacrificed to idols.

1 Now as touching things offered unto idols, we know that we all have knowledge. Knowledge puffeth up, but charity edifieth. 2 And if any man think that he knoweth any thing, he knoweth nothing yet as he ought to know. 3 But if any man love God, the same is known of him.

4 As concerning therefore the eating of those things that are offered in sacrifice unto idols, we know that an idol is nothing in the world, and that there is none other God but one. 5 For though there be that are called gods, whether in heaven or in earth, (as there be gods many, and lords many,) 6 But to us there is but one God, the Father, of whom are all things, and we in him; and one Lord Jesus Christ, by whom are all things, and we by him. 1 CORINTHIANS 8:1-6 (KJV)

Paul starts the discussion by making sure that their consciences are updated to the truth about idols. He does this by pushing aside anything that might be a self-willed opinion concerning the topic of idols. Then Paul explains that an idol is nothing and that there is but one God. Paul goes on to discuss idols as they are perceived by the conscience.

7 Howbeit there is not in every man that knowledge: for some with conscience of the idol unto this hour eat it as a thing offered unto an idol; and their conscience being weak is defiled. 8 But meat commendeth us not to God: for neither, if we eat, are we the better; neither, if we eat not, are we the worse. 1 CORINTHIANS 8:7-8 (KJV)

The weaker brother who does not fully understand idolatry will have a guilty conscience if he eats meat sacrificed to idols. The stronger brother, knowing that an idol is nothing, will not think much about it when he eats. At this point Paul admonishes the stronger to take heed to the conscience of the weaker.

9 But take heed lest by any means this liberty of yours become a stumblingblock to them that are weak. 10 For if any man see thee which hast knowledge sit at meat in the idol's temple, shall not the conscience of him which is weak be emboldened to eat those things which are offered to idols; 11 And through thy knowledge shall the weak brother perish, for whom Christ died? 12 But when ye sin so against the brethren, and wound their weak conscience, ye sin against Christ. 13

Wherefore, if meat make my brother to offend, I will eat no flesh while the world standeth, lest I make my brother to offend. 1 CORINTHIANS 8:9-13 (KJV)

If the weak brother eats, then he is condemned because he cannot do it by faith. Even though the stronger brother knows that he has not done anything wrong in eating, he has sinned in that his weaker brother feels guilty and is stumbled in his faith. This is referred to as a "sin against Christ." In this case, the weaker brother sins because he cannot eat the meat sacrificed to idols by faith, and the stronger brother has sinned because he has stumbled the weaker brother in his faith. Paul made a similar plea to the Romans.

22 Hast thou faith? have it to thyself before God. Happy is he that condemneth not himself in that thing which he alloweth. 23 And he that doubteth is damned if he eat, because he eateth not of faith: for whatsoever is not of faith is sin. ROMANS 14:22-23 (KJV)

We have liberty in Christ, but in all things we are to do good and not evil. James is explicit in this.

17 Therefore to him that knoweth to do good, and doeth it not, to him it is sin. JAMES 4:17 (KJV)

That knowledge depends upon having a conscience that is updated to the truth of the Word of God.

There is much more that could, and should, be said about the conscience. However, integrating the topic into this book would be difficult. The author is planning another project on the conscience following the completion of this book.

CHAPTER NINE

THINGS MISTAKEN FOR SIN

THERE ARE MANY THINGS that are recognized by the world as evil, yet are not in the least way sin. There are various reasons for this, but most often is a result of worldly attractions such as lust, pride, or self-righteousness. They may also be a product of a conscience that is not properly updated, or they may just be fabrications of the imagination. Sadly, Christians have their own brand of "political correctness" within the Church, and this may produce all manner of legalisms that have nothing to do with sin. Whatever the cause, many are falsely accused of some perceived evil that God does not declare to be sin. In some cases, it is just the opposite of what is being required, such as in the case of spanking. As the world gets further from God, the understanding of right and wrong gets corrupted. As a result, good becomes evil and evil becomes good.

BEING OVERWEIGHT

The author comes from a long line of those who have struggled with their weight. Some people can eat anything they want without any hint of weight gain, while others are easily able to regulate their intake to maintain a slim exterior. These people may still die of stroke, diabetes, heart disease, or organ failure. If you are overweight ("over" what being relative in every way), you are often self-righteously declared to be gluttonous by those who have trouble gaining weight. You can starve yourself, spend days fasting and beseeching God, read every book on dieting available, and try every trick thinkable to take those pounds off, only to eventually throw up your hands in frustration. If God made you fat, you are going to be fat. It is not wrong to try and keep your weight down for health and mobility reasons, but being obsessed with your pants size is not a good thing.

I suggest the reader go to the list of Works of the Flesh in Chapter 7 and see if you can find "obesity" listed anywhere. There is an obsession among women in having a Barbie Doll look, and among men as being Mr. Muscles. Self-love (vanity) and covetousness (desiring to look better than someone else) are listed as Works of the Flesh. We are admonished to be careful concerning how we address the eating habits of others.

1 Him that is weak in the faith receive ye, but not to doubtful disputations. 2 For one believeth that he may eat all things: another, who is weak, eateth herbs. 3 Let not him that eateth despise him that eateth not; and let not him which eateth not judge him that eateth: for God hath received him. 4 Who art thou that judgest another man's servant? to his own master he standeth or falleth. Yea, he shall be holden up: for God is able to make him stand.

5 One man esteemeth one day above another: another esteemeth every day alike. Let every man be fully persuaded in his own mind. 6 He that regardeth the day, regardeth it unto the Lord; and he that regardeth not the day, to the Lord he doth not regard it. He that eateth, eateth to the Lord, for he giveth God thanks; and he that eateth not, to the Lord he eateth not, and giveth God thanks. 7 For none of us liveth to himself, and no man dieth to himself. 8 For whether we live, we live unto the Lord; and whether we die, we die unto the Lord: whether we live therefore, or die, we are the Lord's. 9 For to this end Christ both died, and rose, and revived, that he might be Lord both of the dead and living. 10 But why dost thou judge thy brother? or why dost thou set at nought thy brother? for we shall all stand before the judgment seat of Christ. 11 For it is written, As I live, saith the Lord, every knee shall bow to me, and every tongue shall confess to God.

12 So then every one of us shall give account of himself to God. 13 Let us not therefore judge one another any more: but judge this rather, that no man put a stumblingblock or an occasion to fall in his brother's way.

14 I know, and am persuaded by the Lord Jesus, that there is nothing unclean of itself: but to him that esteemeth any thing to be unclean, to him it is unclean. 15 But if thy brother be grieved with thy meat, now walkest thou not charitably. Destroy not him with thy meat, for whom Christ died. 16 Let not then your good be evil spoken of: 17 For the kingdom of God is not meat and drink; but righteousness, and peace, and joy in the Holy Ghost. 18 For he that in these things serveth Christ is acceptable to God, and approved of men. ROMANS 14:1-19 (KJV)

It is also important for conscience sake not to belittle or look down on those who are overweight. Everyone's metabolism is different. Some are skinny and some are fat; few view themselves as perfect. Those who do often do it from the standpoint of vanity, especially those who dress and act in a fashion that makes them more sexually attractive to those whom they will never marry.

SPANKING

Today we live in a world that thinks in opposition to our parents and grandparents. The vast majority of people in the entire world were spanked by their parents when they were young. Today it is considered unloving to spank a child, but this contradicts the admonition of Scripture:

*24 He that spareth his rod hateth his son: but he that loveth him
chasteneth him betimes. PROVERBS 13:24 (KJV)*

Proverbs was written by King Solomon about three thousand years
ago. Although written by a king, it was written as a father to his son. The
Bible considers spanking, and spanking with a stick in particular, as a
very important parental responsibility. Spanking was to be imposed to
deal with childish rebellion.

*15 Foolishness is bound in the heart of a child; but the rod of correction
shall drive it far from him. PROVERBS 22:10 (KJV)*

The rod was used to point the child towards a wiser course of action.

*15 The rod and reproof give wisdom: but a child left to himself bringeth
his mother to shame. PROVERBS 29:15 (KJV)*

It was not considered a last resort, nor was it a choice among many
for discipline.

*12 Apply thine heart unto instruction, and thine ears to the words of
knowledge. 13 Withhold not correction from the child: for if thou beatest
him with the rod, he shall not die. 14 Thou shalt beat him with the rod,
and shalt deliver his soul from hell. PROVERBS 23:12-14 (KJV)*

Child discipline is to be applied well before there is no hope of
changing behavior.

*18 Chasten thy son while there is hope, and let not thy soul spare for
his crying. PROVERBS 19:18 (KJV)*

For those thinking that spanking is not very gracious and is very legalistic, you are correct in every way. Spanking is 100% law. When a child is born, they are not saved and therefore have no internal restraint of the Holy Spirit. Law needs to be applied until a point of accountability can be reached so that the child can make up their own minds about their relationship to God through Jesus Christ. That is exactly the sense given by the Apostles Paul's instructions to the Galatian Church.

> 23 But before faith came, we were kept under the law, shut up unto the faith which should afterwards be revealed. 24 Wherefore the law was our schoolmaster to bring us unto Christ, that we might be justified by faith. 25 But after that faith is come, we are no longer under a schoolmaster. GALATIANS 4:23-25 (KJV)

The phrase "bring us unto Christ" may be better translated as "bring us up to the point of Christ" The law has never led anyone to salvation nor is salvation, by the law. But before salvation, our actions are all judged by the law as to whether or not we meet the expectations of God. The same is true with a child. Good parents have expectations of their children, and spanking reinforces those expectations as punishment for not meeting expectations. There are at least three expectations that parents have that need reinforcement:

1. The expectation and encouragement for a child not to do something that would hurt them, such as run out into the street or touch a hot stove.

2. The expectation that they will obey household rules.

3. The expectation that their behavior will be good and not bad.

Those who think that spanking is evil would probably think that the chastening of the Lord is also evil, but we find just the opposite in the book of Proverbs as Solomon writes to his son:

> 11 My son, despise not the chastening of the LORD; neither be weary of his correction: 12 For whom the LORD loveth he correcteth; even as a father the son in whom he delighteth. PROVERBS 3:11-12 (KJV)

There are those who would probably say that this is just Old Testament legalism, but the New Testament is not silent on the subject.

> 5 And ye have forgotten the exhortation which speaketh unto you as unto children, My son, despise not thou the chastening of the Lord, nor faint when thou art rebuked of him: 6 For whom the Lord loveth he chasteneth, and scourgeth every son whom he receiveth. 7 If ye endure chastening, God dealeth with you as with sons; for what son is he whom the father chasteneth not? 8 But if ye be without chastisement, whereof all are partakers, then are ye bastards, and not sons. 9 Furthermore we have had fathers of our flesh which corrected us, and we gave them reverence: shall we not much rather be in subjection unto the Father of spirits, and live? 10 For they verily for a few days chastened us after their own pleasure; but he for our profit, that we might be partakers of his holiness. 11 Now no chastening for the present seemeth to be joyous, but grievous: nevertheless afterward it yieldeth the peaceable fruit of righteousness unto them which are exercised thereby. HEBREWS 12:5-12 (KJV)

If God has no expectations for you, then you are not a legitimate son of God. We have a loving Heavenly Father, and He will deal with us as a loving Father would His children. Noting the word "scourge" in verse 6, Vine has this to say about it:

> *2. mastigoo (μαστιγόω, 3146), akin to mastix (see below), is used (a)
> as mentioned under No. 1; (b) of Jewish "scourgings," Matt. 10:17 and
> 23:34; (c) metaphorically, in Heb. 12:6, of the "chastening" by the Lord
> administered in love to His spiritual sons.*
>
> *Note: The Jewish method of "scourging," as described in the Mishna, was
> by the use of three thongs of leather, the offender receiving thirteen stripes
> on the bare breast and thirteen on each shoulder, the "forty stripes save
> one," as administered to Paul five times (2 Cor. 11:24).*[1]

Raising children without expectations is like setting a rudderless boat adrift in the ocean. With no moorings, navigation, propulsion, or purpose, the boat is worse than useless. If you want your children to succeed in life you will have reinforced expectations of them spiritually, morally, physically, and mentally.

HAVING A LARGE FAMILY

It is often frowned upon to have a large number of children. The Bible puts no such limitation on family size.

> *3 Lo, children are an heritage of the Lord: and the fruit of the womb is
> his reward. 4 As arrows are in the hand of a mighty man; so are children
> of the youth. 5 Happy is the man that hath his quiver full of them: they
> shall not be ashamed, but they shall speak with the enemies in the gate.*
> *PSALMS 127:3-5 (KJV)*

The Bible encourages large families and has from the beginning;

> *27 So God created man in his own image, in the image of God created
> he him; male and female created he them. 28 And God blessed them,*

and God said unto them, Be fruitful, and multiply, and replenish the earth, and subdue it: and have dominion over the fish of the sea, and over the fowl of the air, and over every living thing that moveth upon the earth. GENESIS 1:27-28 (KJV)

The command to be fruitful and multiply is very explicit. In this pragmatic world, there are two types of parents: those who believe that children are a liability, and those who view children as a blessing from God. If you believe children are a liability, you will have as many as you can afford. If you believe children are a blessing from God, you will have as many children as the Lord provides. With abortion and birth control at an all-time high, it is apparent that many view children as more than just a liability. They view children as a hinderance to career or an annoyance to a promiscuous life style. Others on the outside are condemning of large families because there is a perceived cost to society as a whole. In any case, there is no good reason to limit family size because it may be perceived as sinful or irresponsible. Those who trust God should never worry about the size of their families.

NAME CALLING AND FIGURES OF SPEECH

While it is true that hostility, ingratitude, and incivility seem to be on the rise, the Bible gives us many examples of name calling and derogatory figures of speech that are considered to be within the bounds of proper discourse. The Lord Jesus gave us several examples of this, and below is one of His more lengthy discourses.

13 But woe unto you, scribes and Pharisees, <u>hypocrites!</u> for ye shut up the kingdom of heaven against men: for ye neither go in yourselves, neither suffer ye them that are entering to go in. 14 Woe unto you, scribes and

Pharisees, <u>hypocrites!</u> for ye devour widows' houses, and for a pretence make long prayer: therefore ye shall receive the greater damnation. 15 Woe unto you, scribes and Pharisees, <u>hypocrites!</u> for ye compass sea and land to make one proselyte, and when he is made, ye make him <u>twofold</u> more the <u>child of hell</u> than yourselves. 16 Woe unto you, ye <u>blind guides</u>, which say, Whosoever shall swear by the temple, it is nothing; but whosoever shall swear by the gold of the temple, he is a debtor! 17 <u>Ye fools</u> and blind: for whether is greater, the gold, or the temple that sanctifieth the gold? 18 And, Whosoever shall swear by the altar, it is nothing; but whosoever sweareth by the gift that is upon it, he is guilty. 19 <u>Ye fools</u> and blind: for whether is greater, the gift, or the altar that sanctifieth the gift? 20 Whoso therefore shall swear by the altar, sweareth by it, and by all things thereon. 21 And whoso shall swear by the temple, sweareth by it, and by him that dwelleth therein. 22 And he that shall swear by heaven, sweareth by the throne of God, and by him that sitteth thereon. 23 Woe unto you, scribes and Pharisees, <u>hypocrites!</u> for ye pay tithe of mint and anise and cummin, and have omitted the weightier matters of the law, judgment, mercy, and faith: these ought ye to have done, and not to leave the other undone. 24 <u>Ye blind guides, which strain at a gnat, and swallow a camel.</u> 25 Woe unto you, scribes and Pharisees, <u>hypocrites!</u> for ye make clean the outside of the cup and of the platter, but within they are <u>full of extortion and excess.</u> 26 Thou <u>blind</u> Pharisee, cleanse first that which is within the cup and platter, that the outside of them may be clean also. 27 Woe unto you, scribes and Pharisees, <u>hypocrites!</u> for <u>ye are like unto whited sepulchres,</u> which indeed appear beautiful outward, but are within full of dead men's bones, and of all uncleanness. 28 Even so ye also outwardly appear righteous unto men, but within ye are <u>full of hypocrisy and iniquity.</u> 29 Woe unto you, scribes and Pharisees, <u>hypocrites!</u> because ye build the tombs of the prophets, and garnish the sepulchres of the righteous, 30 And say, If we had been in the days of our fathers, we would not have been partakers *with them in the blood of the prophets. 31 Wherefore ye be witnesses unto yourselves, that ye are the children of them which killed the prophets. 32 Fill ye up then the measure of your fathers. 33 <u>Ye serpents, ye generation of vipers</u>, how can ye escape the damnation of hell? MATTHEW 13:23-33 (KJV) (underlined emphasis added)*

Hypocrites, whitened sepulchers full of dead men's bones, blind guides, two-fold children of Hell, damned, serpents, vipers, and full of iniquity are all seen in this passage to describe the Scribes and the Pharisees. These were the religious leaders in Jesus' day. The term "hypocrites" was used at least nine times. There were also some phrases used, such as "Woe unto you," "children of them that kill the prophets," and those who "strain at a gnat and swallow a camel." To say that the Lord was not happy with religious leadership is an understatement. Jesus was not alone. The Apostle Paul had his confrontations as well.

8 But Elymas the sorcerer (for so is his name by interpretation) withstood them, seeking to turn away the deputy from the faith. 9 Then Saul, (who also is called Paul,) filled with the Holy Ghost, set his eyes on him, 10 And said, O full of all subtilty and all mischief, thou child of the devil, thou enemy of all righteousness, wilt thou not cease to pervert the right ways of the Lord? 11 And now, behold, the hand of the Lord is upon thee, and thou shalt be blind, not seeing the sun for a season. And immediately there fell on him a mist and a darkness; and he went about seeking some to lead him by the hand. 12 Then the deputy, when he saw what was done, believed, being astonished at the doctrine of the Lord. ACTS 13:8-12 (KJV)

Paul used the descriptive phrase "Oh full of all subtilty and mischief" and followed it by calling Elymus "thou child of the Devil" and "thou enemy of all righteousness." Finally, he laid his charge, "Wilt thou not cease to pervert the right way of the Lord?" This was followed by Elymus being struck blind. For those who think such a thing could have no purpose, it said that the local leader believed. This is not what most people would do for evangelism, but it worked in this case.

The Apostle Peter weighed in to the name calling, devoting an entire chapter to the description of false teachers:

1 But there were false prophets also among the people, even as there shall be false teachers among you, who privily shall bring in damnable heresies, even denying the Lord that bought them, and bring upon themselves swift destruction. 2 And many shall follow their pernicious ways; by reason of whom the way of truth shall be evil spoken of. 3 And through covetousness shall they with feigned words make merchandise of you: whose judgment now of a long time lingereth not, and their damnation slumbereth not.

4 For if God spared not the angels that sinned, but cast them down to hell, and delivered them into chains of darkness, to be reserved unto judgment; 5 And spared not the old world, but saved Noah the eighth person, a preacher of righteousness, bringing in the flood upon the world of the ungodly; 6 And turning the cities of Sodom and Gomorrha into ashes condemned them with an overthrow, making them an ensample unto those that after should live ungodly; 7 And delivered just Lot, vexed with the filthy conversation of the wicked: 8 (For that righteous man dwelling among them, in seeing and hearing, vexed his righteous soul from day to day with their unlawful deeds;) 9 The Lord knoweth how to deliver the godly out of temptations, and to reserve the unjust unto the day of judgment to be punished: 10 But chiefly them that walk after the flesh in the lust of uncleanness, and despise government. Presumptuous are they, selfwilled, they are not afraid to speak evil of dignities. 11 Whereas angels, which are greater in power and might, bring not railing accusation against them before the Lord.

12 But these, as natural brute beasts, made to be taken and destroyed, speak evil of the things that they understand not; and shall utterly perish in their own corruption; 13 And shall receive the reward of unrighteousness, as they that count it pleasure to riot in the day time. Spots they are and blemishes, sporting themselves with their own deceivings while they feast with you; 14 Having eyes full of adultery, and that cannot cease from sin; beguiling unstable souls: an heart they have exercised with covetous practices; cursed children: 15 Which have forsaken the right way, and are gone astray, following the way of Balaam the son of Bosor, who loved the wages of unrighteousness; 16 But was rebuked for his iniquity: the dumb ass speaking with man's voice forbad the madness of the prophet.

17 These are wells without water, clouds that are carried with a tempest; to whom the mist of darkness is reserved for ever.

18 For when they speak great swelling words of vanity, they allure through the lusts of the flesh, through much wantonness, those that were clean escaped from them who live in error. 19 While they promise them liberty, they themselves are the servants of corruption: for of whom a man is overcome, of the same is he brought in bondage. 20 For if after they have escaped the pollutions of the world through the knowledge of the Lord and Saviour Jesus Christ, they are again entangled therein, and overcome, the latter end is worse with them than the beginning. 21 For it had been better for them not to have known the way of righteousness, than, after they have known it, to turn from the holy commandment delivered unto them. 22 But it is happened unto them according to the true proverb, The dog is turned to his own vomit again; and the sow that was washed to her wallowing in the mire. 1 PETER 2:1-22 (KJV)

This lengthy passage stands on its own. Jude also gave a lengthy description of those who would pervert the truth:

3 Beloved, when I gave all diligence to write unto you of the common salvation, it was needful for me to write unto you, and exhort you that ye should earnestly contend for the faith which was once delivered unto the saints. 4 For there are certain men crept in unawares, who were before of old ordained to this condemnation, ungodly men, turning the grace of our God into lasciviousness, and denying the only Lord God, and our Lord Jesus Christ.

5 I will therefore put you in remembrance, though ye once knew this, how that the Lord, having saved the people out of the land of Egypt, afterward destroyed them that believed not. 6 And the angels which kept not their first estate, but left their own habitation, he hath reserved in everlasting chains under darkness unto the judgment of the great day. 7 Even as Sodom and Gomorrha, and the cities about them in like manner, giving themselves over to fornication, and going after strange flesh, are set forth for an example, suffering the vengeance of eternal fire.

8 Likewise also these filthy dreamers defile the flesh, despise dominion, and speak evil of dignities. 9 Yet Michael the archangel, when contending with the devil he disputed about the body of Moses, durst not bring against him a railing accusation, but said, The Lord rebuke thee. 10 But these speak evil of those things which they know not: but what they know naturally, as brute beasts, in those things they corrupt themselves. 11 Woe unto them! for they have gone in the way of Cain, and ran greedily after the error of Balaam for reward, and perished in the gainsaying of Core.

12 These are spots in your feasts of charity, when they feast with you, feeding themselves without fear: clouds they are without water, carried about of winds; trees whose fruit withereth, without fruit, twice dead, plucked up by the roots; 13 Raging waves of the sea, foaming out their own shame; wandering stars, to whom is reserved the blackness of darkness for ever.

14 And Enoch also, the seventh from Adam, prophesied of these, saying, Behold, the Lord cometh with ten thousands of his saints, 15 To execute judgment upon all, and to convince all that are ungodly among them of all their ungodly deeds which they have ungodly committed, and of all their hard speeches which ungodly sinners have spoken against him.

16 These are murmurers, complainers, walking after their own lusts; and their mouth speaketh great swelling words, having men's persons in admiration because of advantage. 17 But, beloved, remember ye the words which were spoken before of the apostles of our Lord Jesus Christ; 18 How that they told you there should be mockers in the last time, who should walk after their own ungodly lusts. 19 These be they who separate themselves, sensual, having not the Spirit. JUDE 1:3-19 (KJV)

These lengthy descriptions of hypocritical leaders, blasphemers, false teachers, and trouble makers are enough to let us know that there are occasions when name calling is warranted. Not only name calling, but providing colorful descriptions of their evil deeds as well. Though things of this nature should probably be done sparingly, it is evident that they have their place. If the name calling needs to apply, it needs to be accurate in description, and it needs to promote a movement towards the truth. The same is true of using descriptive phrases.

BEING FALSELY ACCUSED BY FRIENDS

America appears to be obsessed with the idea of "karma." That is, the notion that all our evils are revisited upon us. This is expressed as, "What goes around, comes around." The Bible does have a concept called "sowing and reaping," but it does not follow us after we die, as Hindu "karma" does.

> 7 Be not deceived; God is not mocked: for whatsoever a man soweth, that shall he also reap. 8 For he that soweth to his flesh shall of the flesh reap corruption; but he that soweth to the Spirit shall of the Spirit reap life everlasting. 9 And let us not be weary in well doing: for in due season we shall reap, if we faint not. GALATIANS 6:6-9 (KJV)

Sowing and reaping can include either good or bad. As Dr. Charles Stanley is fond of saying, "You reap what you sow, you reap more than you sow, and you reap later than you sow."[2] Whatever similarities there are between "karma" and "sowing and reaping" are purely incidental, though both assume evil for evil, and good for good.

Yet not everything is due to cause and effect. Jesus' disciples asked Him about a blind man that He had healed and about who had sinned to cause the blindness.

> 1 And as Jesus passed by, he saw a man which was blind from his birth. 2 And his disciples asked him, saying, Master, who did sin, this man, or his parents, that he was born blind? 3 Jesus answered, Neither hath this man sinned, nor his parents: but that the works of God should be made manifest in him. JOHN 9:1-3 (KJV)

Immediately following this Jesus healed the blind man. Even so, not all our trials and tribulations are brought about because we have sinned. Some are indeed sowing and reaping, others are because of the sins of others, and others are simply to demonstrate the glory of God. All of these should be viewed as opportunities for spirituality. Unfortunately, there are inevitably those who are more than willing to declare any brother guilty of some imagined sin that has nothing to do with the problems at hand. We have an excellent example of this with Job.

According to Job Chapters 1 and 2, after the Lord had allowed Satan to kidnap Job's help, steal his livestock, kill many of his servants, and kill all of his children, Satan was allowed by God to smite Job with boils from head to foot. Job was a very sickly and miserable man, but in all this Job did not bring accusation against God. He was a much better man than the author.

While Job sat at home in misery, he was visited by three friends: Eliphaz the Temanite, and Bildad the Shuhite, and Zophar the Naamathite. These men were some of the worst friend imaginable. Eliphaz was the first to condemn Job as bringing this evil upon himself by sowing and reaping.

7 Remember, I pray thee, who ever perished, being innocent? or where were the righteous cut off? 8 Even as I have seen, they that plow iniquity, and sow wickedness, reap the same. 9 By the blast of God they perish, and by the breath of his nostrils are they consumed. JOB 4:7-9 (KJV)

This is but a sampling of the diatribe. Then it was Bildad's turn and he was no comfort in the loss of job's children.

2 How long wilt thou speak these things? and how long shall the words of thy mouth be like a strong wind? 3 Doth God pervert judgment? or doth the Almighty pervert justice? 4 If thy children have sinned against him, and he have cast them away for their transgression; 5 If thou wouldest seek unto God betimes, and make thy supplication to the Almighty; 6 If thou wert pure and upright; surely now he would awake for thee, and make the habitation of thy righteousness prosperous. JOB 8:2-6 (KJV)

Bildad was every bit as condemning verbose as Eliphaz. Next it was Zophar's turn, and he outright calls Job a liar.

2 Should not the multitude of words be answered? and should a man full of talk be justified? 3 Should thy lies make men hold their peace? and when thou mockest, shall no man make thee ashamed? 4 For thou hast said, My doctrine is pure, and I am clean in thine eyes. 5 But oh that God would speak, and open his lips against thee; 6 And that he would shew thee the secrets of wisdom, that they are double to that which is! Know therefore that God exacteth of thee less than thine iniquity deserveth. JOB 11:2-6 (KJV)

After condemnation, Job is encouraged to make a false confession. With great swelling words, Job is laid waste by his friends for things that were neither of his making nor under his control. Finally, God intervenes.

1 Then the Lord answered Job out of the whirlwind, and said, 2 Who is this that darkeneth counsel by words without knowledge? JOB 38:1-2 (KJV)

God explains to Job that even though he had done nothing he is still inferior to the Almighty. Job repented of his unbelief. Then God turned to Job's friends.

7 And it was so, that after the Lord had spoken these words unto Job, the Lord said to Eliphaz the Temanite, My wrath is kindled against thee, and against thy two friends: for ye have not spoken of me the thing that is right, as my servant Job hath. 8 Therefore take unto you now seven bullocks and seven rams, and go to my servant Job, and offer up for yourselves a burnt offering; and my servant Job shall pray for you: for him will I accept: lest I deal with you after your folly, in that ye have not spoken of me the thing which is right, like my servant Job. 9 So Eliphaz the Temanite and Bildad the Shuhite and Zophar the Naamathite went, and did according as the Lord commanded them: the Lord also accepted Job. JOB 42:7-9

Then God healed Job and returned to him more than he had taken. This is actually a story with a good ending for all. Unfortunately, there are many friends just like Job's friends who insist that people are hiding some deep, dark sin that cannot be named and cannot be proven. These people make accusations about things they know nothing about. Instead of being an encouragement, they are a detriment to healing and reconciliation. They are without compassion, without reason, and without any sense of judgment. Still, many of them are otherwise good friends.

There is a judicial concept that states one is innocent until proven guilty. If a charge cannot even be brought, declaring a general state of guilt is counterproductive at best, and a damnable lie at worst. Encouraging a brother to repent of known sin is one thing. Making it up as you go along is quite another.

TEMPTATIONS

Temptations are not sin, but often people are judged as if they have done something wrong in being tempted. Succumbing to the temptation is sin. Job was initially tempted by the Devil, but he did not sin.

22 In all this Job sinned not, nor charged God foolishly. JOB 1:22 (KJV)

Jesus was tempted of the Devil three times in the wilderness but did not sin. The Matthew account is given below. We have already studied the Luke account.

1 Then was Jesus led up of the Spirit into the wilderness to be tempted of the devil. 2 And when he had fasted forty days and forty nights, he was afterward an hungred. 3 And when the tempter came to him, he said, If thou be the Son of God, command that these stones be made bread. 4 But he answered and said, It is written, Man shall not live by bread alone, but by every word that proceedeth out of the mouth of God. 5 Then the devil taketh him up into the holy city, and setteth him on a pinnacle of the temple, 6 And saith unto him, If thou be the Son of God, cast thyself down: for it is written, He shall give his angels charge concerning thee: and in their hands they shall bear thee up, lest at any time thou dash thy foot against a stone. 7 Jesus said unto him, It is written again, Thou shalt not tempt the Lord thy God. 8 Again, the devil taketh him up into an exceeding high mountain, and sheweth him all the kingdoms of the world, and the glory of them; 9 And saith unto him, All these things will I give thee, if thou wilt fall down and worship me. 10 Then saith Jesus unto him, Get thee hence, Satan: for it is written, Thou shalt worship the Lord thy God, and him only shalt thou serve. 11 Then the devil leaveth him, and, behold, angels came and ministered unto him. MATTHEW 4:1-11 (KJV)

In all this, Jesus did not sin. The desire to sin may be present in a temptation. If that were not the case, then it would not be tempting. The fulfilment of the act is up to the individual and his reliance upon the Lord. As was mentioned in the Luke account of the first temptation, chemical reactions were going on in the Lord's body that are normal to anyone. He had not eaten for forty days and He was hungry. Hunger is produced by enzymes in the stomach that tell us we need to eat. When we fail to eat, the enzymes do not just stop telling us we are hungry. The same may be true of sexual arousal or sleep. That does not mean we are to be ruled by our hormones in anger or any other sin. Those who overcome such things should be applauded. The fact that God made man to eat, God made man to sleep, God made man to reproduce, and God made man to have feelings is not wrong in itself. What we do with these feelings in using them improperly for the purpose of sin is all important.

PART THREE

Victory Above the Battle

THIS WORLD IS NOT MY HOME

A Folk Hymn

1. This world is not my home I'm just passing through
my treasures are laid up somewhere beyond the blue
the angels beckon me from Heaven's open door
and I can't feel at home in this world anymore

Chorus

O Lord you know I have no friend like you
if Heaven's not my home then Lord what will I do?
the angels beckon me from Heaven's open door
and I can't feel at home in this world anymore

2. They're all expecting me and that's one thing I know
my savior pardoned me and now I onward go
I know He'll take me through though I am weak and poor|
and I can't feel at home in this world anymore

Chorus

O Lord you know I have no friend like you
if Heaven's not my home then Lord what will I do?
the angels beckon me from Heaven's open door
and I can't feel at home in this world anymore

3. Just up in Glory Land we'll live eternally
the Saints on every hand are shouting victory
their song of sweetest praise drifts back from Heaven's shore|
and I can't feel at home in this world anymore

Chorus

O Lord you know I have no friend like you
if Heaven's not my home then Lord what will I do?
the angels beckon me from Heaven's open door
and I can't feel at home in this world anymore

CHAPTER TEN

LIFE IN THE SPIRIT

As the Song says, "This World Is Not My Home." We are in this World, but our citizenship is in Heaven.

> *20 For our conversation **(citizenship or community)** is in heaven; from whence also we look for the Saviour, the Lord Jesus Christ: 21 Who shall change our vile body, that it may be fashioned like unto his glorious body, according to the working whereby he is able even to subdue all things unto himself. PHILIPPIANS 3:20-21 (KJV)*

But while we are here, we are strangers and pilgrims in a strange land. We must live a life by the Holy Spirit in order to navigate through this world until we reach the next. The spiritual life is all about our deliverance from sin in this world, both the Satanic World System and the Present Evil Age. It is sin that keeps us from fellowship with God. That deliverance was at great cost to our Lord a great deal of pain and suffering, but the result was a glorious opportunity for us to be close to Him. Such opportunity also invokes a cost on our part. We must be willing to submit our trust and will to the Lord. This does not result in an easier path through life, but it is a more bearable path. In fact, the believer is promised anything but smooth sailing through life. As Jesus said of our relationship to the World:

18 If the world hate you, ye know that it hated me before it hated you. 19 If ye were of the world, the world would love his own: but because ye are not of the world, but I have chosen you out of the world, therefore the world hateth you. JOHN 15:18-19 (KJV)

Our suffering is even compared to the World.

12 Yea, and all that will live godly in Christ Jesus shall suffer persecution. 13 But evil men and seducers shall wax worse and worse, deceiving, and being deceived. 2 TIMOTHY 3:12-13 (KJV)

But the relationship that we have with God is sure because we are indwelled by God as His holy temple.

16 Know ye not that ye are the temple of God, and that the Spirit of God dwelleth in you? 17 If any man defile the temple of God, him shall God destroy; for the temple of God is holy, which temple ye are. 1 CORINTHIANS 3:16-17 (KJV)

We are not to use our bodies as a device of sin, in this case not for fornication. Again it says of the Temple of God:

19 What? know ye not that your body is the temple of the Holy Ghost which is in you, which ye have of God, and ye are not your own? 20 For ye are bought with a price: therefore glorify God in your body, and in your spirit, which are God's. 1 CORINTHIANS 6:19-20 (KJV)

Jesus gave us the promise of the Spirit's coming, as has been mentioned. As God's Holy Temple, our bodies belong to Him. They are bought and paid for. Our bodies as believers are also to be maintained for the Lord.

1 I beseech you therefore, brethren, by the mercies of God, that ye present your bodies a living sacrifice, holy, acceptable unto God, which is your reasonable service. 2 And be not conformed to this world: but be ye transformed by the renewing of your mind, that ye may prove what is that good, and acceptable, and perfect, will of God. ROMANS 12:1-2 (KJV)

After such a passage, one would expect to see dietary restrictions and rules for healthy living. Instead, it talks about the care and feeding of the spiritual man. If the spiritual man is accommodated, the physical man will follow as required. In order to assist us in our spiritual growth, God allows us to go through trials and temptations for our benefit.

6 Wherein ye greatly rejoice, though now for a season, if need be, ye are in heaviness through manifold temptations: 7 That the trial of your faith, being much more precious than of gold that perisheth, though it be tried with fire, might be found unto praise and honour and glory at the appearing of Jesus Christ: 8 Whom having not seen, ye love; in whom, though now ye see him not, yet believing, ye rejoice with joy unspeakable and full of glory: 9 Receiving the end of your faith, even the salvation of your souls. 1 PETER 1:6-9 (KJV)

It is in suffering that we are truly partakers of Christ's suffering.

12 Beloved, think it not strange concerning the fiery trial which is to try you, as though some strange thing happened unto you: 13 But rejoice, inasmuch as ye are partakers of Christ's sufferings; that, when his glory shall be revealed, ye may be glad also with exceeding joy. 14 If ye be reproached for the name of Christ, happy are ye; for the spirit of glory and of God resteth upon you: on their part he is evil spoken of, but on your part he is glorified. 1 PETER 4:12-14 (KJV)

Such suffering we have as we encounter our Spiritual Enemies, the Flesh within and the Devil and his world system without. There are several things to remember concerning our Spiritual Enemies. These are enemies that are ever present, but not seen. Even the World that we see is manipulated by forces that it knows nothing about. Our primary source of knowledge about these enemies is the Bible and the Bible alone. This is what the Bible has to say about our life in dealing with these unseen foes.

EVERY PHYSICAL TRIAL IS A SPIRITUAL BATTLE

The Devil will never walk up to you and say, "Hi, I'm the Devil and I'm here to tempt you." The trials that we have are allowed by God, and the Devil will not go past what he is allowed to do, but what he is allowed to do is almost never good. It may be pleasurable in the short term, as much sin is, but it will not be good. Our trials may look and feel earthly, and the Devil may use others against us, but our battles are really spiritual in nature.

> 12 For we wrestle not against flesh and blood, but against principalities, against powers, against the rulers of the darkness of this world, against spiritual wickedness in high places. EPHESIANS 6:12 (KJV)

As we have read, Job probably did not know that what he had experienced was of the Devil's doing. Eve was deceived by a serpent not knowing that the Devil was behind it. And so, it is with all of us.

EVERY SPIRITUAL BATTLE IS ALSO A SPIRITUAL OPPORTUNITY

These spiritual battles are also spiritual opportunities.

1 Therefore being justified by faith, we have peace with God through our Lord Jesus Christ: 2 By whom also we have access by faith into this grace wherein we stand, and rejoice in hope of the glory of God. 3 And not only so, but we glory in tribulations also: knowing that tribulation worketh patience; 4 And patience, experience; and experience, hope: 5 And hope maketh not ashamed; because the love of God is shed abroad in our hearts by the Holy Ghost which is given unto us. ROMANS 5:1-5 (KJV)

Our spiritual battles are allowed by God to build our character.

2 My brethren, count it all joy when ye fall into divers temptations; 3 Knowing this, that the trying of your faith worketh patience. 4 But let patience have her perfect work, that ye may be perfect and entire, wanting nothing. JAMES 1:2-4 (KJV)

We are being fitted for Heaven and for Eternity Future. By the time God is finished with us He expects perfection because He is willing and able to achieve it.

24 Now unto him that is able to keep you from falling, and to present you faultless before the presence of his glory with exceeding joy, 25 To the only wise God our Saviour, be glory and majesty, dominion and power, both now and ever. Amen. JUDE 1:24-25 (KJV)

ALL SPIRITUAL BATTLES ARE LIMITED BY GOD

Trials seem scary, but we need not be overwhelmed. God knows our limits and has promised us that He will not let those limits be exceeded.

12 Wherefore let him that thinketh he standeth take heed lest he fall. 13 There hath no temptation taken you but such as is common to man: but God is faithful, who will not suffer you to be tempted above that ye are able; but will with the temptation also make a way to escape, that ye may be able to bear it. 1 CORINTHIANS 10:12-13 (KJV)

God will never put us in a position where our faith will fail. We are not guaranteed that we will not suffer physically, nor emotionally. We may even be very embarrassed at times. We may even suffer the loss of all worldly possessions and relationships. But God is faithful and He will limit it to whatever we can take. He can do this because He supplies the grace to get us through. Romans chapter eight gives one of the best explanations for that grace.

THE HOLY SPIRIT IS MORE POWERFUL THAN OUR FLESH

In Chapter 2, we looked at the power of the Flesh and how it wars against the Spirit. We found that the only thing that can control the Flesh is the Holy Spirit of God. Not even willpower is sufficient to overcome the Flesh. Romans declares this power of the Spirit to be a law with the axiom that the Spirit will set us free from the law of sin and death.

1 There is therefore now no condemnation to them which are in Christ Jesus, who walk not after the flesh, but after the Spirit. 2 For the law of the Spirit of life in Christ Jesus hath made me free from the law of sin and death. 3 For what the law could not do, in that it was weak through the flesh, God sending his own Son in the likeness of sinful flesh, and for sin, condemned sin in the flesh: 4 That the righteousness of the law might be fulfilled in us, who walk not after the flesh, but after the Spirit. 5 For they that are after the flesh do mind the things of the flesh; but they that are after the Spirit the things of the Spirit. 6 For to be carnally minded is death; but to be spiritually minded is life and peace. 7 Because the carnal mind is enmity against God: for it is not subject to the law of God, neither indeed can be. 8 So then they that are in the flesh cannot please God. ROMANS 8:1-8 (KJV)

The Holy Spirit sets our minds free from the evils of our own sin nature. As always, the battleground is in the mind. The mind controlled of God overcomes sin. The mind controlled by the Flesh delights in sin. The passage goes on to remind us that the operation of the Holy Spirit dwelling within the believer is an ongoing operation. This is what it means to walk by the Spirit. Those who do not are enemies with God.

9 But ye are not in the flesh, but in the Spirit, if so be that the Spirit of God dwell in you. Now if any man have not the Spirit of Christ, he is none of his. 10 And if Christ be in you, the body is dead because of sin; but the Spirit is life because of righteousness. 11 But if the Spirit of him that raised up Jesus from the dead dwell in you, he that raised up Christ from the dead shall also quicken your mortal bodies by his Spirit that dwelleth in you. ROMANS 8:9-11 (KJV)

Prior to salvation we were dead to God and separated from Him. After salvation we receive the Holy Spirit, and we are dead to sin and alive to God, even as Christ was raised from the dead.

GOD CARES FOR US AS HIS CHILDREN

The fact that we are made alive to God and indwelled by the Holy Spirit gives the believer a new position with God. We are no longer enemies, and we are certainly more than friends. We are made a part of God's family and declared to be Sons of God. While we were at one time frightened by God, we now may call Him "Daddy."

> 12 Therefore, brethren, we are debtors, not to the flesh, to live after the flesh. 13 For if ye live after the flesh, ye shall die: but if ye through the Spirit do mortify the deeds of the body, ye shall live. 14 For as many as are led by the Spirit of God, they are the sons of God. 15 For ye have not received the spirit of bondage again to fear; but ye have received the Spirit of adoption, whereby we cry, Abba, Father. 16 The Spirit itself beareth witness with our spirit, that we are the children of God: 17 And if children, then heirs; heirs of God, and joint-heirs with Christ; if so be that we suffer with him, that we may be also glorified together. ROMANS 8:12-17 (KJV)

As with many prominent earthly families, our placement into God's family gives us an inheritance. As we suffer with Christ we become joint heirs with Jesus. So, our suffering becomes a vehicle to closeness with God.

THE HOLY SPIRIT INTERCEDES FOR US

As Children of God we have access to Him, but we do not always know what is best for us. God always knows and the Holy Spirit will ask for us.

> 26 Likewise the Spirit also helpeth our infirmities: for we know not what we should pray for as we ought: but the Spirit itself maketh intercession for us with groanings which cannot be uttered. 27 And he that searcheth the hearts knoweth what is the mind of the Spirit, because he maketh intercession for the saints according to the will of God. ROMANS 8:26-27 (KJV)

God does not sit on the sidelines when it comes to the saints as His children. The Holy Spirit is always active on our behalf.

WE ALWAYS HAVE ACCESS TO GOD

Our access to God is bolstered by the fact that Jesus is now our advocate and He makes intercession for us as well.

> 1 My little children, these things write I unto you, that ye sin not. And if any man sin, we have an advocate with the Father, Jesus Christ the righteous: 2 And he is the propitiation for our sins: and not for ours only, but also for the sins of the whole world. 1 JOHN 2:1-2 (KJV)

Because Jesus has paid the price for our sins, we also, may now come boldly to God. In the Old Testament ,only the High Priest could go before God once a year, but not without sacrifice. Because Jesus made a once for-all-time sacrifice for our sins and presented His Own Blood at the altar of God in Heaven, we have that same privilege of coming to God.

> 14 Seeing then that we have a great high priest, that is passed into the heavens, Jesus the Son of God, let us hold fast our profession. 15 For we have not an high priest which cannot be touched with the feeling of our infirmities; but was in all points tempted like as we are, yet without sin. 16 Let us therefore come boldly unto the throne of grace, that we may obtain mercy, and find grace to help in time of need. HEBREWS 4:14-16 (KJV)

God is always there and we always have access to Him, either by the Holy Spirit, or by the Lord Jesus Christ as our advocate and High Priest, or personally because of Jesus' finished work on Calvary's Cross. God is there for us.

> 5 Let your conversation be without covetousness; and be content with such things as ye have: for he hath said, I will never leave thee, nor forsake thee. 6 So that we may boldly say, The Lord is my helper, and I will not fear what man shall do unto me. HEBREWS 13:5-6 (KJV)

This knowledge should encourage the believer and help us not to worry. We have an all-powerful, all-knowing, and everywhere-present God. He is not up in Heaven wringing His hands and wondering what is going to happen to us. If God is not worried, then why should we worry? As before mentioned in Chapter 3, worry is a Satanic temptation. The Devil wants us to believe that he is as powerful as God, or that God is not very powerful. As with most things that the Devil does, it is a lie.

GOD HAS A PLAN

God does not work in a haphazard manner, nor are His actions by random chance. God never guesses at what to do next. As His children, He has a plan for us as well. As the first chapter of Ephesians tells us:

> *3 Blessed be the God and Father of our Lord Jesus Christ, who hath blessed us with all spiritual blessings in heavenly places in Christ: 4 According as he hath chosen us in him before the foundation of the world, that we should be holy and without blame before him in love: 5 Having predestinated us unto the adoption of children by Jesus Christ to himself, according to the good pleasure of his will, 6 To the praise of the glory of his grace, wherein he hath made us accepted in the beloved. EPHESIANS 1:3-6 (KJV)*

And

> *11 In whom also we have obtained an inheritance, being predestinated according to the purpose of him who worketh all things after the counsel of his own will: 12 That we should be to the praise of his glory, who first trusted in Christ. EPHESIANS 1:11-12 (KJV)*

If we are predestined according to His counsel and His will, then our destiny is predetermined by God. We may not always take the best path in getting there because we are not programmable robots without free will, but God knows where we need to go and what we need to do to get there. As a result, God is able to work everything out for our benefit.

> 28 And we know that all things work together for good to them that love God, to them who are the called according to his purpose. 29 For whom he did foreknow, he also did predestinate to be conformed to the image of his Son, that he might be the firstborn among many brethren. 30 Moreover whom he did predestinate, them he also called: and whom he called, them he also justified: and whom he justified, them he also glorified. ROMANS 8:28-30 (KJV)

God's ultimate plan for all His children is that they become just like Jesus. Not that we become God, but that in all our actions we reflect the attributes of God and become godly in every way. If we are willing to follow it, that plan is already worked out.

WHATEVER WE SUFFER GOD WILL ALWAYS LOVE US

As stated before, God's plan for our lives does not mean that we are not going to suffer. Even as the Lord told Ananias about the future of the Apostle Paul:

> 15 But the Lord said unto him, Go thy way: for he is a chosen vessel unto me, to bear my name before the Gentiles, and kings, and the children of Israel: 16 For I will shew him how great things he must suffer for my name's sake. ACTS 9:15-16 (KJV)

Why should any believer be exempt from such things? Jesus suffered and died for all our sins. Should He not be our example? But even as the Father was with Christ, so God shall be with us.

31 What shall we then say to these things? If God be for us, who can be against us? 32 He that spared not his own Son, but delivered him up for us all, how shall he not with him also freely give us all things? 33 Who shall lay any thing to the charge of God's elect? It is God that justifieth. 34 Who is he that condemneth? It is Christ that died, yea rather, that is risen again, who is even at the right hand of God, who also maketh intercession for us. 35 Who shall separate us from the love of Christ? shall tribulation, or distress, or persecution, or famine, or nakedness, or peril, or sword? 36 As it is written, For thy sake we are killed all the day long; we are accounted as sheep for the slaughter. ROMANS 8:31-36 (KJV)

We will always be delivered in our trials and temptations because God loves us. We may be wounded, we may be ridiculed, we may be falsely accused, and we may even be killed, but we are guaranteed that it will always work out for our benefit.

THE LOVE OF GOD IS INESCAPABLE

We can have a victorious Christian life over temptation, trials, and tribulations, but only as we see the source of the victory as coming from God. God does this because He loves His children. As the following passage says, that love is inescapable.

37 Nay, in all these things we are more than conquerors through him that loved us. 38 For I am persuaded, that neither death, nor life, nor angels, nor principalities, nor powers, nor things present, nor things to come, 39 Nor height, nor depth, nor any other creature, shall be able to separate us from the love of God, which is in Christ Jesus our Lord. ROMANS 8:37-39 (KJV)

With the help of Romans Chapter 8, and a few other passages, the spiritual life has been summarized. We know that we are God's possession and that His goal is the perfecting of the saints. We know that He does this for our benefit and that He loves us. We also know that no effort for the Lord is wasted. All of this depends upon the attitudes we will study in the next chapter called "the Fruit of the Spirit." There are a few more things we must consider.

THE KEYS TO SPIRITUAL VICTORY ARE TRUST IN GOD AND THANKFULNESS

Trust in God is paramount. Salvation past, present, and future are through Jesus and it is all according to the plan of God. If we decide to take on our Spiritual Enemies on our own, we will fail. If we try another plan other than God's plan, we will fail. From the Garden of Eden to the present, man has considered himself smarter than God, and it has cost him dearly. As the Proverb says:

> 5 Trust in the Lord with all thine heart; and lean not unto thine own understanding. 6 In all thy ways acknowledge him, and he shall direct thy paths. 7 Be not wise in thine own eyes: fear the Lord, and depart from evil. PROVERBS 3:5-7 (KJV)

But man does not trust in God and his flesh will not let him depart from evil. The biggest reason for a failure to trust God is that man is not thankful.

> 16 Rejoice evermore. 17 Pray without ceasing. 18 In every thing give thanks: for this is the will of God in Christ Jesus concerning you. 1 THESSALONIANS 5:16-18 (KJV)

Giving thanks in "everything" is a tall order. Most of us would be no different than Job in considering his great losses: his servants, his livelihood, and all his children. Yet God did not forsake Job and He will not forsake us. As it is written of Job:

> 20 Then Job arose, and rent his mantle, and shaved his head, and fell down upon the ground, and worshipped, 21 And said, Naked came I out of my mother's womb, and naked shall I return thither: the Lord gave, and the Lord hath taken away; blessed be the name of the Lord. 22 In all this Job sinned not, nor charged God foolishly. JOB 1:20-22 (KJV)

Our attitude should be even as Job, thankful to God for what he had while he had it. But we have even greater promises by the Holy Spirit.

> 9 But as it is written, Eye hath not seen, nor ear heard, neither have entered into the heart of man, the things which God hath prepared for them that love him. 10 But God hath revealed them unto us by his Spirit: for the Spirit searcheth all things, yea, the deep things of God. 1 CORINTHIANS 2:9-10 (KJV)

NEVER TRY TO GET EVEN

As a last warning, some trials and temptations are worse than others and some are very painful. The greater temptation is to view these spiritual battles as strictly earthly and personal. Earth may be where they take place, and they indeed happen to us making them seem personal, but those who do evil are but pawns of a greater and more sinister unseen power. The tendency is generally to get even. The Scriptures warn against it, especially among the brethren.

> 8 Finally, be ye all of one mind, having compassion one of another, love as brethren, be pitiful, be courteous: 9 Not rendering evil for evil,

or railing for railing: but contrariwise blessing; knowing that ye are thereunto called, that ye should inherit a blessing. 1 PETER 3:8-9 (KJV)

There will still be evil men who are unsaved. For them we have a very strong promise from God, and a greater responsibility as well.

17 Recompense to no man evil for evil. Provide things honest in the sight of all men. 18 If it be possible, as much as lieth in you, live peaceably with all men. 19 Dearly beloved, avenge not yourselves, but rather give place unto wrath: for it is written, Vengeance is mine; I will repay, saith the Lord. 20 Therefore if thine enemy hunger, feed him; if he thirst, give him drink: for in so doing thou shalt heap coals of fire on his head. 21 Be not overcome of evil, but overcome evil with good. ROMANS 12:17-21 (KJV)

Our duty is to the living and to a lost and dying world. We must be kind as much as lies within us. But for those who insist of being evil to the end:

30 For we know him that hath said, Vengeance belongeth unto me, I will recompense, saith the Lord. And again, The Lord shall judge his people. 31 It is a fearful thing to fall into the hands of the living God. HEBREWS 10:30-31 (KJV)

The evil and the unrepentant God reserves for judgment. We need not do it for Him.

CHAPTER ELEVEN

THE VIRTUES AND ATTITUDES OF GRACE

GOD MAKES PROVISION for the believer beyond anything that can be seen or imagined. The supernatural nature of this was explained in Chapter 2 with our defense against the Flesh and the internal restraint of the Holy Spirit. Again, in Chapter 3 the supernatural nature of the Armor of God was explained as a defense against the Devil. In this chapter, the method of the Holy Spirit's restraint is examined. The "Fruit of the Spirit" is a supernatural set of virtues and attitudes that give the believer assistance in overcoming the Works of the Flesh that were detailed in Chapter 8. Being "of the Spirit," these virtues and attitudes cannot be manufactured by man or any device of man. They are a reflection of the attributes of God in man. They are given by God to keep the believer from sin.

> *22 But the fruit of the Spirit is love, joy, peace, longsuffering, gentleness, goodness, faith, 23 Meekness, temperance: against such there is no law. 24 And they that are Christ's have crucified the flesh with the affections and lusts. 25 If we live in the Spirit, let us also walk in the Spirit. GALATIANS 5:22-25 (KJV)*

Even though these attitudes are given by God, they should not be confused with the "Gifts of the Spirit" which are given for service.

4 Now there are diversities of gifts, but the same Spirit. 5 And there are differences of administrations, but the same Lord. 6 And there are diversities of operations, but it is the same God which worketh all in all. 7 But the manifestation of the Spirit is given to every man to profit withal. 8 For to one is given by the Spirit the word of wisdom; to another the word of knowledge by the same Spirit; 9 -- To another faith by the same Spirit; to another the gifts of healing by the same Spirit; 10 -- To another the working of miracles; to another prophecy; to another discerning of spirits; to another divers kinds of tongues; to another the interpretation of tongues: 11 But all these worketh that one and the selfsame Spirit, dividing to every man severally as he will. 1 CORINTHIANS 12:4-11 (KJV)

Diversity of Spiritual Gifts is given for the edification of the Body of Christ, the Church.

12 Even so ye, forasmuch as ye are zealous of spiritual gifts, seek that ye may excel to the edifying of the church. 1 CORINTHIANS 14:12 (KJV)

As we look at the segment of Spiritual Fruit called "love," we will gain a better understanding of how the spiritual life is more to be desired than Spiritual Gifts. Unlike Spiritual Gifts, the Fruit of the Spirit exhibited in man resembles in every way the attributes and characteristics of God.

LOVE (AGAPE)

There are several Greek words for "love" used in the New Testament, but the word for sexual love, **eros**, is not found. Four other words used are for love:[1]

Phileo – Brotherly love

Philanthropia – Acts of kindness

Philafguria – The love of money

Agape – Love of a perfect being given to an entirely unworthy object

Phileo and *agape* are sometimes confused. Some have even suggested that they have an identical meaning and should be used interchangeably. However, only *agape* is used as a part of the Fruit of the Spirit. Vine gives more weight to the separation of the two words.

> 2. phileo (φιλέω, 5368) is to be distinguished from agapao in this, that phileo more nearly represents "tender affection." The two words are used for the "love" of the Father for the Son, John 3:35 (No. 1), and 5:20 (No. 2); for the believer, 14:21 (No. 1) and 16:27 (No. 2); both, of Christ's "love" for a certain disciple, 13:23 (No. 1), and 20:2 (No. 2). Yet the distinction between the two verbs remains, and they are never used indiscriminately in the same passage; if each is used with reference to the same objects, as just mentioned, each word retains its distinctive and essential character.[2]

Since the Fruit of the Spirit reflects God's character in man, it would be nice to see **agape** love reflected as an attribute of God in Scripture. We do have such a reflection:

> 7 Beloved, let us love one another: for love is of God; and every one that loveth is born of God, and knoweth God. 8 He that loveth not knoweth not God; for God is love. 1 JOHN 4:7-8 (KJV)

At first glance, the statement "for God is love" appears to be a definition. However, without an article present to make the statement definitive, a better translation would be "for a quality (or attribute) of God is love." This is exactly what we are looking for. Notice also that this love is said to be "of God" and is exhibited by those who are "born of God" and who "know God." Conversely, those who do not exhibit love do not know God. If that is the case, then what is this love supposed to look like? We have an entire chapter of the Bible to explain it to us. The preface to this passage follows a chapter on Spiritual Gifts:

> 31 But covet earnestly the best gifts: and yet shew I unto you a more excellent way. 1 CORINTHIANS 12:31 (KJV)

1 Corinthians 13, the "love chapter," starts out with a discussion of Spiritual Gifts that are mistaken for love (in this case translated as the word "charity" in the King James).

> 1 Though I speak with the tongues of men and of angels, and have not charity, I am become as sounding brass, or a tinkling cymbal. 2 And though I have the gift of prophecy, and understand all mysteries, and all knowledge; and though I have all faith, so that I could remove mountains, and have not charity, I am nothing. 3 And though I bestow all my goods to feed the poor, and though I give my body to be burned, and have not charity, it profiteth me nothing. 1 CORINTHIANS 13:1-3 (KJV)

This tells us that the Spiritual Life is more to be desired than Spiritual Gifts. This is as it should be. The one is a gift of service towards others, while the other is an actual attribute of God. It should be noted that nowhere in this passage is there a command to love as we see in 1 John. The passage is a picture of what love looks like so we may know it when we see it. If this love is truly "of God" then it is not subject to artificial manufacture by man. God is the only one who can produce it. The passage goes on with a description of love.

4 Charity suffereth long, and is kind; charity envieth not; charity vaunteth not itself, is not puffed up, 5 Doth not behave itself unseemly, seeketh not her own, is not easily provoked, thinketh no evil; 6 Rejoiceth not in iniquity, but rejoiceth in the truth; 7 Beareth all things, believeth all things, hopeth all things, endureth all things. 1 CORINTHIANS 13:4-7 (KJV)

It should be noted that other segments of the Fruit of the Spirit, such as joy, gentleness, meekness, long suffering, and temperance, are imbedded in the definition of love. Love appears to be the bedrock of the other segments of the Fruit of the Spirit. Such ideas as "innocent until proven guilty" also come from this passage. At the same time, it does not give place to evil. The passage goes on with a discussion of the inferiority of certain Spiritual Gifts to love:

8 Charity never faileth: but whether there be prophecies, they shall fail; whether there be tongues, they shall cease; whether there be knowledge, it shall vanish away. 9 For we know in part, and we prophesy in part. 10 But when that which is perfect is come, then that which is in part shall be done away.

11 When I was a child, I spake as a child, I understood as a child, I thought as a child: but when I became a man, I put away childish things. 12 For now we see through a glass, darkly; but then face to face: now I know in part; but then shall I know even as also I am known. 1 CORINTHIANS 13:8-12 (KJV)

Even the loaned abilities for service that we receive from God are inferior to the character of God exhibited in the Fruit of the Spirit. The abilities granted will last only so long as they serve a purpose, but God in all His glory will abide forever, as will His character. That is the statement of the last verse in the passage:

> *13 And now abideth faith, hope, charity, these three; but the greatest of these is charity. 1 CORINTHIANS 13:13 (KJV)*

Faith is mentioned in this chapter as both a Spiritual Gift and as a character attribute. It is also mentioned in the book of Ephesians as a God-supplied piece of the Armor of God for defense against the Devil. But faith is still inferior to love. Hope is not mentioned in Galatians 5 as a part of the Fruit of the Spirit, but it is keeping company with both love and faith. Therefore, "hope" appears to have similar qualities to the Fruit of the Spirit in that it is said to be "abiding" or long lasting. Hope will be examined at the end of this chapter as a characteristic related to God.

Love is also integral as a defense against the Satanic World System.

> *15 Love not the world, neither the things that are in the world. If any man love the world, the love of the Father is not in him. 16 For all that is in the world, the lust of the flesh, and the lust of the eyes, and the pride of life, is not of the Father, but is of the world. 17 And the world passeth away, and the lust thereof: but he that doeth the will of God abideth for ever. 1 JOHN 2:15-17 (KJV)*

As a spiritual enemy, the World, with its many attractions to the senses, will pull the believer away from the things of the Spirit and towards the snares of lust and pride. The result is that the believer no longer directs his God given attribute of love towards the things of God. Instead he directs his love towards the World. The result is sin in all of its various forms.

There are 142 uses of the verb form **agapaō** [3] and 116 uses of the noun form of love **agapē** [4]. A further study is advised as there is too much material available for this narrow study.

JOY (CHARA)

Joy (**chara**) is used 59 times in the New Testament.[5] Joy is another attribute of God expressed as an attitude. This was demonstrated by the angels at the birth of our Lord.

> *10 And the angel said unto them, Fear not: for, behold, I bring you good tidings of great joy, which shall be to all people. 11 For unto you is born this day in the city of David a Saviour, which is Christ the Lord. 12 And this shall be a sign unto you; Ye shall find the babe wrapped in swaddling clothes, lying in a manger. 13 And suddenly there was with the angel a multitude of the heavenly host praising God, and saying, 14 Glory to God in the highest, and on earth peace, good will toward men. LUKE 2:10-14 (KJV)*

Joy not only brings a sense of gladness, it also brings exuberance, a sense of thrill and adventure. It could be compared to detective novels like Nancy Drew, the Hardy Boys, or the Ivan series. The heroes always found themselves in some sort of trouble, and it was always thrilling to see how they were going to get out of it. As a characteristic of God to keep believers from sin, joy is the attitude that takes the drudgery out of trials and temptations. The author has friends in the engineering contracting business. The work normally requires travel and moving frequently. A dear Christian lady who is the wife of one of these contracts would always say just before a move, "Well, it is off to another adventure with the Lord." This is a very good example of God-given Christian joy. In this case it was a trial, but the same is true of temptations. As James tells us:

2 My brethren, count it all joy when ye fall into divers temptations; 3 Knowing this, that the trying of your faith worketh patience. 4 But let patience have her perfect work, that ye may be perfect and entire, wanting nothing. JAMES 1:2-4 (KJV)

Joy (**chara**) is closely related to rejoice (**chairo**).[6] The Lord Jesus used "rejoice" in the Sermon on the Mount to describe the believer's attitude under persecution.

11 Blessed are ye, when men shall revile you, and persecute you, and shall say all manner of evil against you falsely, for my sake.

12 Rejoice, and be exceeding glad: for great is your reward in heaven: for so persecuted they the prophets which were before you. MATTHEW 5:11-12 (KJV)

The Lord knows our trials and, if we are steadfast, we will receive a proper reward for it. Rejoicing is also a command.

16 Rejoice evermore. 17 Pray without ceasing. 18 In every thing give thanks: for this is the will of God in Christ Jesus concerning you. 1 THESSALONIANS 5:16-18 (KJV)

Why else would it be God's will for us to rejoice and to pray were it not a part of His character?

PEACE (EIRĒNĒ)

Eirēnē means "to join" and is associated with a lack of conflict, as in peace between nations.[7] It describes the peace we have with God as a result of our reconciliation through the Cross.

1 Therefore being justified by faith, we have peace with God through our Lord Jesus Christ: ROMANS 5:1 (KJV)

Peace is the opposite of disorder.

33 For God is not the author of confusion, but of peace, as in all churches of the saints. 1 CORINTHIANS 14:33 (KJV)

Peace, as the absence of conflict, is a unifying factor.

11 Finally, brethren, farewell. Be perfect, be of good comfort, be of one mind, live in peace; and the God of love and peace shall be with you. 2 CORINTHIANS 13:11 (KJV)

Peace is the attribute of God that allows for forgiveness and reconciliation. Because we have peace with God, we have access to Him. But those who have not the Spirit of God are at war continually with God because of sin.

6 For to be carnally minded is death; but to be spiritually minded is life and peace. 7 Because the carnal mind is enmity against God: for it is not subject to the law of God, neither indeed can be. 8 So then they that are in the flesh cannot please God. ROMANS 8:6-8 (KJV)

Our access to God is assured by the finished work of Jesus Christ. The fact that Jesus died for our sins and nailed our sin nature to the Cross with Him allows us to draw close to a holy and perfect God.

14 For he is our peace, who hath made both one, and hath broken down the middle wall of partition between us; 15 Having abolished in his flesh the enmity, even the law of commandments contained in ordinances;

for to make in himself of twain one new man, so making peace; 16 And
that he might reconcile both unto God in one body by the cross, having
slain the enmity thereby: 17 And came and preached peace to you which
were afar off, and to them that were nigh. 18 For through him we both
have access by one Spirit unto the Father. EPHESIANS 2:14-18 (KJV)

Believers are to have the same attitude as God in our dealings with others. It is this attitude of peace that allows the believer to be forgiving toward others in times of trial and temptation. If this were not the case, ,then vengeance and evil payback would surely be the attitude of the Flesh.

14 Follow peace with all men, and holiness, without which no man shall
see the Lord: HEBREWS 12:14 (KJV)

Peace is integral to the Christian life. The Apostle Paul started most of his epistles with the same appeal of **"Grace to you and peace from God the Father and our Lord Jesus Christ."** It is peace from God, which mean that it is peace supplied by God.

LONG SUFFERING (MAKROTHYMIA)

The verb form, **makrothumeo**, is generally translated as "patience,"[8] and the adverb form, **makrothumos**, is translated as "patiently."[9] Twelve out of fourteen occurrences of the noun used for the segment of the Fruit of the Spirit, **makrothymia**, are translated as "longsuffering." It is defined as patience, endurance, constancy, steadfastness, perse-verance, forbearance, and slowness in avenging wrongs.[10] Occurrences in Scripture have it associated with many other word translated as "forbearance" and "patience." The Apostle Peter gives us a glimpse of how God is longsuffering.

18 For Christ also hath once suffered for sins, the just for the unjust, that he might bring us to God, being put to death in the flesh, but quickened by the Spirit: 19 By which also he went and preached unto the spirits in prison; 20 Which sometime were disobedient, when once the longsuffering of God waited in the days of Noah, while the ark was a preparing, wherein few, that is, eight souls were saved by water. 21 The like figure whereunto even baptism doth also now save us (not the putting away of the filth of the flesh, but the answer of a good conscience toward God,) by the resurrection of Jesus Christ: 1 PETER 3:18-21 (KJV)

In the days of Noah, man was evil and God was not happy about it.

5 And God saw that the wickedness of man was great in the earth, and that every imagination of the thoughts of his heart was only evil continually. 6 And it repented the Lord that he had made man on the earth, and it grieved him at his heart. 7 And the Lord said, I will destroy man whom I have created from the face of the earth; both man, and beast, and the creeping thing, and the fowls of the air; for it repenteth me that I have made them. 8 But Noah found grace in the eyes of the Lord. GENESIS 6:5-8 (KJV)

God was longsuffering in the days of Noah and waited for Noah to build the Ark before He exacted judgement upon the world. That wait was not short.

3 And the Lord said, My spirit shall not always strive with man, for that he also is flesh: yet his days shall be an hundred and twenty years. GENESIS 6:3 (KJV)

The reason for the wait was to save Noah and his family.

7 By faith Noah, being warned of God of things not seen as yet, moved with fear, prepared an ark to the saving of his house; by the which he condemned the world, and became heir of the righteousness which is by faith. HEBREWS 11:7 (KJV)

In longsuffering, God stuck to His plan of making a way for man to escape judgment. The Ark only saved eight people to repopulate the Earth, but God's plan for Noah paved the way all the way to the Cross for Jesus to provide our ultimate salvation from sin. Both God and Noah persevered in the face of evil: Noah by faith and God by promise. The sense given for longsuffering is similar to what the military refers to as "coolness under fire." In the midst of destruction, it is still necessary to achieve the objectives and stick to the plan to achieve them. This is what we see concerning God and His plan for us.

22 What if God, willing to shew his wrath, and to make his power known, endured with much longsuffering the vessels of wrath fitted to destruction: 23 And that he might make known the riches of his glory on the vessels of mercy, which he had afore prepared unto glory, 24 -- Even us, whom he hath called, not of the Jews only, but also of the Gentiles? ROMANS 9:19-24 (KJV)

Thus, the segment of the Fruit of the Spirit known as longsuffering is not only patience, it is also an attitude that is not frustrated by circumstance. Man, in his flesh, would often panic.

GENTLENESS (CHRESTOTES)

Chrestotes is often translated as "goodness." It means righteous or of high moral quality. It is also translated as "kindness."[11] Translated as "good," it is used in describing our shortcomings before a holy and righteous God, Romans 11:22 specifically.

12 They are all gone out of the way, they are together become unprofitable; there is none that doeth good, no, not one. ROMANS 3:12 (KJV)

Because of sin, moral goodness is something that man falls short of producing on his own. In describing the inclusion of the gentiles into the household of faith, Paul describes our position as resulting from the goodness of God.

19 Thou wilt say then, The branches were broken off, that I might be grafted in. 20 Well; because of unbelief they were broken off, and thou standest by faith. Be not highminded, but fear: 21 For if God spared not the natural branches, take heed lest he also spare not thee. 22 Behold therefore the goodness and severity of God: on them which fell, severity; but toward thee, goodness, if thou continue in his goodness: otherwise thou also shalt be cut off. 23 And they also, if they abide not still in unbelief, shall be grafted in: for God is able to graff them in again. ROMANS 11:19-23 (KJV)

Our goodness is dependent upon our faith. If we are unbelieving, we are cut off. This demonstrates that goodness has a content of belief. If you do not believe the right things, you will not be spared by God. Goodness is thus supplied by God.

4 Or despisest thou the riches of his goodness and forbearance and longsuffering; not knowing that the goodness of God leadeth thee to repentance? ROMANS 2:4 (KJV)

Translated as "kindness," we see ***chrestotes*** as a manifestation of God's grace to maintain our salvation.

7 That in the ages to come he might shew the exceeding riches of his grace in his kindness toward us through Christ Jesus. EPHESIANS 2:7 (KJV)

This is also true of the initial work of salvation found in Titus.

3 For we ourselves also were sometimes foolish, disobedient, deceived, serving divers lusts and pleasures, living in malice and envy, hateful, and hating one another. 4 But after that the kindness and love of God our Saviour toward man appeared, 5 Not by works of righteousness which we have done, but according to his mercy he saved us, by the washing of regeneration, and renewing of the Holy Ghost; TITUS 3:3-5 (KJV)

Chrestotes is a quality of kind virtue that is not normally exhibited by those outside the faith. But it is a quality that is always exhibited by God and is part of His basis for our salvation—past, present, and future.

GOODNESS (AGATHŌSYNĒ)

Agathōsynē is a word that is always translated as "goodness."[12] It differs from chrestotes in what it describes. Where ***chrestotes*** described moral quality, ***agathōsynē*** describes characteristic quality. As an example, an apple may taste good, but it has no moral sense, even if it were stolen. The "goodness" in the verse below could mean full of good qualities or virtues.

14 And I myself also am persuaded of you, my brethren, that ye also are full of goodness, filled with all knowledge, able also to admonish one another. ROMANS 15:14 (KJV)

These qualities are also active and they produce good things. In the following verse, what is produced is what is acceptable to the Lord.

> 8 For ye were sometimes darkness, but now are ye light in the Lord: walk as children of light: 9 (For the fruit of the Spirit is in all goodness and righteousness and truth;) 10 Proving what is acceptable unto the Lord. EPHESIANS 5:6 (KJV)

It is also used of God and the good things that He produces.

> 11 Wherefore also we pray always for you, that our God would count you worthy of this calling, and fulfil all the good pleasure of his goodness, and the work of faith with power: 2 THESSALONIANS 1:11 (KJV)

Agathōsynē is the quality of doing good and having good characteristics, as opposed to **chrestotes** the quality of being morally good and having good character. It is like a carpenter with pride in his work. He does good work because it reflects his skills. Even so, God supplies the believer with a set of skills to overcome sin.

FAITH (PISTIS)

There is only one word for faith, **pistis**, but it carries a multitude of implications. Faith and belief are the same word.[13] The verb form of the word, **pistos**, is translated as faithful, faithfully, believe, believing, sure, or true.[14] The *Strong's Dictionary* definitions are extensive. They list belief about God, belief about Christ, Christian belief, trust in God, those who exhibit faithfulness and reliability. None relate a belief instilled by God as an attitude or attribute of God. Nor is there anything about the Shield of Faith supplied by God as a defense against the Devil.

PISTIS

1. *conviction of the truth of anything, belief; in the NT of a conviction or belief respecting man's relationship to God and divine things, generally with the included idea of trust and holy fervor born of faith and joined with it*

   a. *relating to God the conviction that God exists and is the creator and ruler of all things, the provider and bestower of eternal salvation through Christ*

   b. *relating to Christ a strong and welcome conviction or belief that Jesus is the Messiah, through whom we obtain eternal salvation in the kingdom of God*

   c. *the religious beliefs of Christians*

   d. *belief with the predominate idea of trust (or confidence) whether in God or in Christ, springing from faith in the same*

2. *fidelity, faithfulness the character of one who can be relied on*

Vine has verbiage but no more enlightenment. But it may be possible to use what the Bible has to say about faith to give examples of where the faith of the believer was reinforced by God. We start with how faith is described:

1 Now faith is the substance of things hoped for, the evidence of things not seen. 2 For by it the elders obtained a good report. 3 Through faith we understand that the worlds were framed by the word of God, so that things which are seen were not made of things which do appear. HEBREWS 11:1-3 (KJV)

From verse 1 we see that faith is evidence and has substance, or content. From verse 3 we see that faith provides understanding or knowledge about the operations of God. What is left is to see where God has supplied evidence or knowledge. In this case we are looking at things of the Holy Spirit supplied by God that we are assured are meant for the believer. First of all, we know that in our trials and temptations we are not under the condemnation of God.

1 There is therefore now no condemnation to them which are in Christ Jesus, who walk not after the flesh, but after the Spirit. ROMANS 8:1 (KJV)

We know this by the Spirit of God who is in us.

9 But ye are not in the flesh, but in the Spirit, if so be that the Spirit of God dwell in you. Now if any man have not the Spirit of Christ, he is none of his. 10 And if Christ be in you, the body is dead because of sin; but the Spirit is life because of righteousness. 11 But if the Spirit of him that raised up Jesus from the dead dwell in you, he that raised up Christ from the dead shall also quicken your mortal bodies by his Spirit that dwelleth in you. ROMANS 8:9-11 (KJV)

We know that we are alive to the Spirit because of the finished work of Jesus Christ on Calvary's Cross. We are alive because He has crucified sin in the flesh and made us alive to God. Being alive to the Spirit we can be led of the Spirit.

12 Therefore, brethren, we are debtors, not to the flesh, to live after the flesh. 13 For if ye live after the flesh, ye shall die: but if ye through the Spirit do mortify the deeds of the body, ye shall live. 14 For as many as are led by the Spirit of God, they are the sons of God. ROMANS 8:12-14 (KJV)

Being led of the Spirit as Sons of God we have the added benefit of the direct intervention of God.

15 For ye have not received the spirit of bondage again to fear; but ye have received the Spirit of adoption, whereby we cry, Abba, Father. 16 The Spirit itself beareth witness with our spirit, that we are the children of God: 17 And if children, then heirs; heirs of God, and joint-heirs with Christ; if so be that we suffer with him, that we may be also glorified together. ROMANS 8:15-17 (KJV)

And this is what we need to know about how God supplies our much-needed faith in our times of trials and temptations. It is by means of the Holy Spirit interceding on our behalf. This and much more overlaps with the previous chapter on the Spiritual Life.

MEEKNESS (PRA,OTĒS)

Pra,otēs is used nine times in the New Testament and the King James always renders it as "meekness." Strong's indicates that it is derived from the word for "humility," but does not list it among the synonyms including "gentleness" and "mildness."[15] In other Bible translations, it is commonly rendered as "Humble." Rushton indicates that there is no good English equivalent for the word.[16] **Pra,otēs** is apparently a calm self-assurance that is, in this case, God given.

Meekness is often included in lists of other qualities or segments of Spiritual Fruit (Galatians 5:22-23, Ephesians 4:2, Colossians 3:12, 1 Timothy 6:11). The Apostle Paul used meekness to describe his own attitude towards the Church in Corinth.

1 *Now I Paul myself beseech you by the meekness and gentleness of Christ, who in presence am base among you, but being absent am bold toward you: 2 CORINTHIANS 10:1 (KJV)*

Paul also instructed the Church in Galatia that meekness was the attitude they should have in correcting a brother in the Lord.

1 *Brethren, if a man be overtaken in a fault, ye which are spiritual, restore such an one in the spirit of meekness; considering thyself, lest thou also be tempted. GALATIANS 6:1 (KJV)*

Timothy was also instructed to correct others with an attitude of meekness.

24 *And the servant of the Lord must not strive; but be gentle unto all men, apt to teach, patient, 25 In meekness instructing those that oppose themselves; if God peradventure will give them repentance to the acknowledging of the truth; 26 And that they may recover themselves out of the snare of the devil, who are taken captive by him at his will. 2 TIMOTHY 2:24-26 (KJV)*

Titus was told to be meek in the instruction of unruly brethren concerning good citizenship.

1 *Put them in mind to be subject to principalities and powers, to obey magistrates, to be ready to every good work, 2 To speak evil of no man, to be no brawlers, but gentle, shewing all meekness unto all men. TITUS 2:15 (KJV)*

It appears that **pra,otēs** (meekness) is the attitude necessary for spiritual correction. It would be hoped that this would not be done in any other way but by means of the Holy Spirit.

TEMPERANCE (EGKRATEIA)

Egkrateia is translated all four times that it is used in the King James as "temperance." Strong gives the definition as:[17]

> *self-control (the virtue of one who masters his desires and passions, esp. his sensual appetites)*

Even though it is defined as control by self, it is of the Spirit and must therefore be a God-granted ability to curb the appetites of the Flesh. **Egkrateia** is used among the things spoken of by the Apostle Paul to Felix while Paul was held captive.

> *24 And after certain days, when Felix came with his wife Drusilla, which was a Jewess, he sent for Paul, and heard him concerning the faith in Christ. 25 And as he reasoned of righteousness, temperance, and judgment to come, Felix trembled, and answered, Go thy way for this time; when I have a convenient season, I will call for thee. ACTS 24:24-25 (KJV)*

Temperance is also used by Peter as an attribute of the godly that is not held by the ungodly.

> *5 And beside this, giving all diligence, add to your faith virtue; and to virtue knowledge; 6 And to knowledge temperance; and to temperance patience; and to patience godliness; 7 And to godliness brotherly kindness; and to brotherly kindness charity. 8 For if these things be in you, and abound, they make you that ye shall neither be barren nor unfruitful in the knowledge of our Lord Jesus Christ. 9 But he that lacketh these things is blind, and cannot see afar off, and hath forgotten that he was purged from his old sins. 2 PETER 1:5-9 (KJV)*

As before stated, even though it is defined as control by self, it is of the Spirit and must therefore be a God-granted ability to curb the appetites of the Flesh. This is most important for people having problems with addiction, be they chemical or sexual. People who exhibit addictive behaviors can hardly turn down anything within their addiction. It is God who must intervene ,and we have a promise that He will if we are willing to walk by the Spirit.

HOPE (ELPIS) HAVING SIMILAR QUALITY TO SPIRITUAL FRUIT

Hope is not a segment of the Fruit of the Spirit, but it is mentioned in company with such fruit.

> *13 And now abideth faith, hope, charity, these three; but the greatest of these is charity. 1 CORINTHIANS 13:13 (KJV)*

If "love" and "faith" are the company that "hope" keeps, then it must be similar in quality as the Fruit of the Spirit. Fifty-three out of fifty-four times in the King James Bible, **elpis** is translated as "hope." Only once is it translated as "faith." Hope is the expectation of good or better things to come.[18] Hope is always forward looking. As such it is most notably associated with the return of the Lord Jesus Christ.

> *13 Looking for that blessed hope, and the glorious appearing of the great God and our Saviour Jesus Christ; TITUS 2:13 (KJV)*

Hope is what we did not have before we were saved.

> *12 That at that time ye were without Christ, being aliens from the commonwealth of Israel, and strangers from the covenants of promise, having no hope, and without God in the world: EPHESIANS 2:12 (KJV)*

Hope is what we have in a life beyond this one because of salvation.

5 For the hope which is laid up for you in heaven, whereof ye heard before in the word of the truth of the gospel; COLOSSIANS 1:5 (KJV)

Our hope is by the power of the Holy Spirit.

3 For I testify again to every man that is circumcised, that he is a debtor to do the whole law. 4 Christ is become of no effect unto you, whosoever of you are justified by the law; ye are fallen from grace. 5 For we through the Spirit wait for the hope of righteousness by faith. 6 For in Jesus Christ neither circumcision availeth any thing, nor uncircumcision; but faith which worketh by love. GALATIANS 5:3-5 (KJV)

Hope, experience, and patience are by-products of the trial of our faith and results from the Fruit of the Spirit being placed in our hearts by the Holy Spirit.

1 Therefore being justified by faith, we have peace with God through our Lord Jesus Christ: 2 By whom also we have access by faith into this grace wherein we stand, and rejoice in hope of the glory of God. 3 And not only so, but we glory in tribulations also: knowing that tribulation worketh patience; 4 And patience, experience; and experience, hope: 5 And hope maketh not ashamed; because the love of God is shed abroad in our hearts by the Holy Ghost which is given unto us. ROMANS 5:1-5 (KJV)

Our hope is a consolation for our earthly trials.

7 And our hope of you is stedfast, knowing, that as ye are partakers of the sufferings, so shall ye be also of the consolation. 2 CORINTHIANS 1:7 (KJV)

Hope may not be a segment of the Fruit of the Spirit, but it exists as a result of walking by the Spirit.

CHAPTER TWELVE

CONCLUSIONS

IN THESE TWELVE CHAPTERS, we have examined our Spiritual Enemies and found that they can only be defeated by spiritual means. The Flesh (indwelling sin) could only be defeated by nailing it to the Cross of Jesus Christ (Romans 6). Even afterward, the means of control is not our self-will. It is the Holy Spirit of God (Galatians 5:16-17). The Devil was found to be much more of an opponent than earthy man could imagine. Satan can only be defeated by the supernatural Armor of God (Ephesians 6:10-18). We are not to attack the Devil, but simply stand against him and allow the Lord to defeat him. We found that the Devil controls the Satanic World System and that it has enticements for the believer to pull him out of fellowship with God. The defense against the World is to guard our God-given love and not direct it towards worldly things (1 John 2:15-16). God will not give His love over to evil. Then we looked at the physical situation that believers find themselves in in This Present Evil Age (Galatians 1:4). Next we looked at sin itself as a Work of the Flesh. Finally, we looked at the ultimate defense of the Spirit, which is God's fruit, revealed to us as virtues and attitudes that we may manifest with His assistance. These are attributes of God manifested in man.

Our battles are difficult because we tend to view them as physical when they are in fact spiritual. It is much easier to confront something that you can see and understand. It is more difficult to trust God to supply the answers and defeat the enemies of our souls. The key to all is trusting God for victory over sin in the present just as we trusted in Him in the past for our initial salvation from sin. God never stops delivering us, if we let him. We have limited power in ourselves to overcome our own sin nature by any external restraint of law.

We face these battles not because God is a bully, but because God loves us enough to train us for dependence on Him for an eternity. God uses every trial, temptation, and tribulation as a means of spiritual opportunity for us to grow in our relationship with Him. Even in our failures we are brought closer to Him. In the battle for the hearts and souls of men, our troubles are what God uses in His boot camp to make us fit for glory in Heaven.

END NOTES

CHAPTER 1

1. Morgan, Robert J.; *Then Sings My Soul, Book 3*; Nashville, TN: Thomas Nelson, Inc., 2011; pages 31-35.
2. Strong, James; *Strong's Exhaustive Concordance of the Bible*; Nashville, TN: Thomas Nelson, Inc., 1920; Enhanced by Olive Tree Bible Software, Spokane, WA: Number g5046 (*teleios*).

CHAPTER 2

1. Ibid.: Number g3364 from 3756 and 3361 (*ou me*).
2. Chafer, Lewis Sperry; *He That Is Spiritual*; Grand Rapids, MI: Dunham Publishing Company, 1964; pages 150-151.
3. Op. Cit.: Strong, James; Number 3670 (*homologeo*).
4. Ibid.: Number 2075 (*este*).
5. Ibid.: Number 4982 (*sozo*).
6. Note: Ephesians 2:8-10 is not without its controversy. Some versions, such as the English Standard Version, translate the passage in the past tense, tying it to initial salvation. Other versions, such as the King James Version, translate the passage in the present tense, tying it to the spiritual life of the believer. The verb "are" in verse 10 is in the present indicative tense. The verbs "created," "ordained," and "walk" are all in the Aorist tense, making them even more subjective.

CHAPTER 3

1. Chafer, Lewis Sperry; *Satan*; Grand Rapids, MI: Dunham Publishing Company, 1919; page 20.
2. Op. Cit.: Strong, James; Number 1754 (*energeo*).
3. Ibid.: Number 3180 (*methodeia*).

4. Ibid.: Number 3540 (*noema*).

5. Ibid.: Number 3803 (*pagis*).

6. Rushton, Warren H.; *The Maturing Christian and His Enemies*; Thesis Masters of Theology, San Francisco Theological Seminary, 1972.

7. Op. Cit.: Strong, James; Number 165 (*aion*).

8. Ibid.: Number 863 (*aphiemi*).

CHAPTER 4

1. Ibid.: Number 2889 (*kosmos*).

2. Ibid.: Number 165 (*aion*).

3. Ibid.: Number 1754 (*energeo*).

4. Chafer, Lewis Sperry; *Satan*; Grand Rapids, MI: Dunham Publishing Company, 1919; page 44.

5. Op. Cit.: Strong, James; Number 1753 (*energeia*).

CHAPTER 5

1. Ibid.: Number 2889 (*kosmos*).

2. Ibid.: Number 165 (*aion*).

3. *The American Heritage® Dictionary of the English Language*, Fourth Edition, copyright ©2000 by Houghton Mifflin Company. Updated in 2009. Published by Houghton Mifflin Company.

CHAPTER 7

1. Op. Cit.: Strong, James; Number 3430 (*moicheia*).

2. Ibid.: Number 4202 (*porneia*).

3. Ibid.: Number 0167 (*akatharsia*).

4. Ibid.: Number 0766 (*aselgeia*).

5. Vine, W.E.; *An Expository Dictionary of New Testament Words*; Thomas Nelson Publishers, 1984.

6. Ibid.

7. Op. Cit.: Strong, James; Number 5331 (*pharmakeia*).

8. Ibid.: Number 2189 (*echtha*).

9. Ibid.: Number 2054 (*eris*).

10. Ibid.: Number 2205 (*zelos*).

11. Ibid.: Number 2207 (*zelotes*).

12. Ibid.: Number 2372 (*thymos*).

13. Ibid.: Number 2052 (*eritheia*).

14. Ibid.: Number 1370 (*dichostasia*).

15. Ibid.: Number 0139 (*hairesis*).

16. Op. Cit.: Vine, W.E.

17. Ibid.

18. Op. Cit.: Strong, James; Number 5355 (*phthonos*).

19. Ibid.: Number 5408 (*phonos*).

20. Ibid.: Number 3178 (*methē*).

21. Ibid.: Number 2970 (*komos*).

CHAPTER 9

1. Op. Cit.: Vine, W. E.

2. Stanley, Charles; *Life Principles Bible, New King James Version*: Thomas Nelson, Inc., 2005 (NKJV 1982); page 276.

CHAPTER 11

1. Op. Cit.: Vine, W. E.

2. Ibid.

3. Op. Cit.: Strong, James; Number 0025 (*agapaō*).

4. Ibid.: Number 0026 (*agapē*).

5. Ibid.: Number 5479 (*chara*).

6. Op. Cit.: Vine, W. E.

7. Op. Cit.: Strong, James; Number 1515 (*eirēnē*).

8. Ibid.: Number 3114 (*makrothymeō*).

9. Ibid.: Number 3116 (*makrothymōs*).

10. Ibid.: Number 3115 (*makrothymia*).

11. Ibid.: Number 5544 (*chrestotes*).

12. Ibid.: Number 0019 (*agathōsynē*).

13. Ibid.: Number 4102 (*pistis*).

14. Ibid.: Number 4103 (*pistos*).

15. Ibid.: Number 4236 (*pra,otēs*).

16. Op. Cit.: Rushton, Warren H.

17. Op. Cit.: Strong, James; Number 1466 (*egkrateia*).

18. Ibid.: Number 1680 (*elpis*).

CPSIA information can be obtained
at www.ICGtesting.com
Printed in the USA
FFOW03n2121050418
46148099-47296FF